INNOVATING AT THE TOP

think: act
International Management Knowledge series
(launched 2008)

R. Schwientek and A. Schmidt (eds)
OPERATIONS EXCELLENCE
Smart Solutions for Business Success

INSEAD Business Press series
(launched 2006)

J. Frank Brown
THE GLOBAL BUSINESS LEADER
Practical Advice for Success in a Transcultural Marketplace

D. Fubini, C. Price & M. Zollo
MERGERS
Leadership, Performance and Corporate Health

M. Kets de Vries, K. Korotov & E. Florent-Treacy
COUCH AND COUCH
The Psychology of Making Better Leaders

J. Teboul
SERVICE IS FRONT STAGE
Positioning Services for Value Advantage

J. Thoenig & C. Waldman
THE MARKING ENTERPRISE
Business Success and Societal Embedding

INNOVATING AT THE TOP

How Global CEOs Drive Innovation
for Growth and Profit

Roland Berger,
Soumitra Dutta,
Tobias Raffel
& Geoffrey Samuels

INSEAD
Business Press

Roland Berger
Strategy Consultants

palgrave
macmillan

First published 2009 by
PALGRAVE MACMILLAN

Palgrave Macmillan in the UK is an imprint of Macmillan Publishers Limited, registered in England, company number 785998, of Houndmills, Basingstoke, Hampshire RG21 6XS.

Palgrave Macmillan in the US is a division of St Martin's Press LLC, 175 Fifth Avenue, New York, NY 10010.

Palgrave Macmillan is the global academic imprint of the above companies and has companies and representatives throughout the world.

Palgrave® and Macmillan® are registered trademarks in the United States, the United Kingdom, Europe and other countries

ISBN-13: 978–0230–57573–8
ISBN-10: 0–230–57573–0

This book is printed on paper suitable for recycling and made from fully managed and sustained forest sources. Logging, pulping and manufacturing processes are expected to conform to the environmental regulations of the country of origin.

A catalogue record for this book is available from the British Library.

A catalog record for this book is available from the Library of Congress.

10 9 8 7 6 5 4 3 2 1
18 17 16 15 14 13 12 11 10 09

Printed and bound in Great Britain by
Cromwell Press Ltd, Trowbridge, Wiltshire.

CONTENTS

PREFACE

Business and management concepts often cycle through years of favor. Diversification, quality, excellence once occupied the spotlight, then receded to the sidelines to make way for new priorities. Innovation now takes center stage. Is innovation another management "fad," a marketing phrase? Or is innovation fundamentally different, a powerful motor for a globalizing economy? A growing body of data suggests innovation is indeed deeply embedded in the new dynamics of global economic development and competition.

As individuals all involved in both management consulting and academia, we share the view that economic data and statistics confirm that innovation exhibits fundamentally different qualities, more profound and far-reaching than many prior management concepts. Anecdotally, the evidence is overwhelming. At conferences, meetings, and casual encounters, senior executives frequently ask us what can be done to improve innovative performance.

Officers directing companies headquartered on every continent express similar interest and concerns. How to generate better returns from innovation efforts? How to enhance results? How to improve the expenditure–reward equation? We hear these and similar questions more and more. What have we learned in our travels and conversations with senior executives that could shed more light on the mystery of innovation?

Rapid technology development cycles, increased risk,

and faster product rollouts in diverse markets are some of the contemporary trends that "push–pull" innovation, and likely will intensify as globalization spreads. Are conventional views about innovation still valid? Does a company need an innovation culture to be innovative? Must innovation, to paraphrase Hobbes, remain risky, expensive, and long? Are there new methods, policies, and practices that could increase the odds innovation will deliver at least some of its promised rewards?

These questions stirred our interest. We wanted to explore whether there might be useful innovation policies or methods relevant to many companies. So we decided to investigate how highly innovative large corporations across different industries in North America, Europe, and Asia pursue innovation, and interview the people most responsible for the companies' innovative performance, the CEOs.

Because globalization will only increase opportunities and competitive pressures, INSEAD and Roland Berger Strategy Consultants selected highly innovative large global companies to investigate innovation policies and practices that might be highly suggestive and valuable for other companies wishing to compete in global markets.

A high-level CEO perspective is especially revealing because CEOs are uniquely qualified to assess the reasons for their company's innovative performance. Their judgment and views elevated them to the CEO suite. Their opinions distill many years of experience. We considered that an open format where CEOs could discuss their views during an hour-long personal interview would be the most effective way to hear their observations and recommendations.

This volume presents in their own words how CEOs of highly innovative corporations approach the challenge of creating and developing products and services in a world where never before have there been so many opportunities for innovation. Science, improved logistics and communications, expanding markets in developed and emerging countries, demographic shifts, climate change, and energy are the leading drivers opening new innovation frontiers. The innovation policies and practices these CEOs find most effective to pursue these opportunities are a useful guide for other companies looking to create and fill innovative niches.

Innovating at the Top is not an academic survey of all innovation-related activities at each company. The book's purpose is to identify, at a high level, the values and methods the CEO finds most compelling and useful to promote innovation. INSEAD and Roland Berger Strategy Consultants chose the CEOs from the top innovating companies around the world. These CEOs and chairmen raised several issues and attitudes that, while differing in details, intriguingly convey many similar approaches to stimulate innovation. Their views were shared across continents and industries.

The introductory chapter, "CEO innovation perspectives," organizes their observations and recommendations in an overview to highlight important areas of agreement. In the core section of the book, each CEO presents his views on innovation in his own words. This transcript format gives the reader the immediacy of a conversation, and conveys the tone and character of the CEO's comments. This should be helpful to readers for appreciating the nuances and aspects of innovation the CEO considers most important.

While there is no formula for innovation, these interviews make it clear that certain conditions favor innovation and can increase the probability success will reward the considerable efforts innovation requires. The editors sincerely hope this volume of interviews will encourage senior management at other companies to assess their innovation strategy, and consider policies and practices that could, over time, help create a more innovative profile for their company.

Roland Berger,
Soumitra Dutta,
Tobias Raffel
& Geoffrey Samuels

KEY INNOVATION DRIVERS

1. APPOINT THE CEO AS THE INNOVATION CHAMPION

2. CELEBRATE AN INNOVATION CULTURE

3. ENGAGE MORE INNOVATION PARTNERS BY SHARING KNOWLEDGE

4. ORGANIZE DIVERSITY TO PROMOTE POSITIVE FRICTION AND CROSS-FERTILIZATION

5. USE CUSTOMER NEEDS TO DRIVE SIMULTANEOUS R&D AND BUSINESS MODEL INNOVATION

6. SET HIGH-QUALITY STANDARDS AND DEMANDING CHALLENGES

7. ENCOURAGE YOUTH AND KEEP A CHALLENGER MENTALITY

8. APPOINT APPROPRIATE DECISION MAKERS AND ENCOURAGE TRANSPARENT INFORMATION SHARING

9. USE PROCESSES JUDICIOUSLY

10. INCENTIVIZE PEOPLE TO INNOVATE CONTINUOUSLY

CEO INNOVATION PERSPECTIVES

There is no prescription for innovation. This is certainly true, otherwise we should explore why some companies choose not to apply proven formulas for innovative success! But can some conditions increase the probability that a company will produce significant innovations? Are there methods and techniques that could help stimulate innovative performance? Can a company create a fertile ground for innovation?

These questions are particularly apt today because globalization is transforming the pace and stakes of business. If firms wish to compete globally, innovation across the entire spectrum of their activities, products and services, internal organization, and business models, to marketing and customer support, is no longer a choice. It is a competitive imperative. More open global markets, and vastly improved logistics and communication, mean that firms can no longer rely upon traditional sources of competitive advantage, such as specialization, pricing, tariffs, and historical relationships. Globalization speeds product cycles, increases competition, and accelerates market changes. Firms seeking the rewards of global competition must innovate to capture the upside in growing markets.

Because innovation is so important to success, we felt it would be instructive to gain an insight into how some of the world's finest global competitors approach innovation. The editors at INSEAD and Roland Berger Strategy Consultants therefore decided to inquire into the innovative polices and practices at nine large multinationals: 3M, Research in Motion, Genentech, Unilever, SAP, Bosch, Nokia, Infosys, and Toyota. These companies, based in North America, Europe, and Asia, are all widely respected for their innovative skills and track record.

3M is legendary for its range and history of innovation. Research in Motion's Blackberry revolutionized wireless data connectivity. Genentech's record of inventing new medicines and industry firsts is highly admired in the pharmaceutical and biotech industries. Unilever extends the range and market penetration of its consumer products through a balanced strategy of innovation and brand development. SAP pioneered and dominates the enterprise integrated suite software market. Decade after decade Bosch has rolled out innovative products for automobiles and the home.

Nokia, transforming itself by selling off assets unrelated to cellular phone technology, manufactures the world's best-selling mobile communications devices. Infosys founded the Indian IT outsourcing industry and three decades later remains in the fore by continually innovating. *Kaizen*, or continuous improvement, has transformed Toyota into the number one global car manufacturer.

Much has been written about how innovation appears, from theories to motivational tips. While these approaches have their value, we decided to apply a different method. Because the CEO's role in a firm's innovative performance is so important, interviewing the CEO is a particularly useful and direct way to learn about its innovation policies and practices. In addition, the CEO vantage reflects years of experience and judgment, as well as the corporate verdict that these individuals are uniquely qualified to inspire and advance innovation. Because our interview format gave the CEOs the liberty to discuss innovation as they wished, the interviews distill those aspects the CEOs consider to be the most important. Their opinions are not by any means an academic review of all the innovation policies and practices at their companies. This is the benefit of the interviews, because by selecting the issues, the CEOs prioritize and emphasize those aspects of innovation they judge to be the most critical.

The findings? Conditions favoring innovation do indeed exist. What is particularly encouraging is the common ground the CEOs on three continents share across a number of innovation policies and practices, despite different company cultures, business strategies, and ways to weave innovation into their products and services, organization, and business models. Their agreement in so many aspects of innovation strongly suggests that if less innovative companies want to improve their innovative performance, they would do well to review these observations and recommendations.

Of course, creating beneficial conditions for innovation does not imply that successful innovations will appear spontaneously. The CEOs were quite explicit in not raising expectations that if executives enact certain policies, useful innovations will arise as a matter of course. Unexpected developments, delays, wrong turns, and lucky breaks are all part of the process, and the companies have not been immune to failures. However, the cumulative result is that over the years these large corporations have delivered highly innovative products and services into the marketplace.

The following pages discuss in more detail the CEOs' recommended key innovation drivers. A brief note about methodology is relevant here to explain how we identified these drivers. We analyzed the observations and recommendations cited by all the CEOs, and grouped them by subject matter and frequency to find those innovation policies and practices they considered to be most important. Notable, but less frequently mentioned drivers are also included, although less space is devoted to summarizing the comments about them. As previously mentioned, what is striking is the extent to which CEOs in North America, Europe, and Asia agree on so many fundamentals to encourage innovation. This overview chapter then ends by noting common innovation barriers and obstacles.

INNOVATION DRIVERS – RECOMMENDATIONS FROM THE TOP

1. Appoint the CEO as the innovation champion

The days are long past when innovation leadership could be assigned to R&D or marketing departments. All CEO interviewees are quite clear that innovation starts in the CEO's suite. A champion of innovation, the CEO should consistently express and demonstrate their conviction. From George Buckley's, "my main job is to promote innovation," to "setting the tone" expressed by Art Levinson, advancing innovation is a defining feature of CEO leadership. Patrick Cescau advises that the CEO "needs to be clear that it is a top leadership activity, one that needs to be managed from the top." Action is always more important than words. "An innovation culture has to start at the top," advises Franz Fehrenbach. "But only if it is communicated consistently and over a long period of time, and only if it regularly produces good results in practice, will this idea penetrate the whole company – level by level."

The CEOs cite three essential traits for innovation leadership: positive encouragement, a tolerance for failure, and patience. Whether to "create the right framework, the right mindset" at Bosch, or directing "senior leaders to create an environment of friendliness, courtesy, encouragement and helpful attitudes to ... innovative ideas" at Infosys, a supportive attitude towards innovation is essential.

Accepting failure, although not repeating the same errors, is twin to encouraging the innovative stretch. Buckley affirms, "You have to accept that [failure], take it for what it's worth, learn from it and move on." Cescau agrees: "if you don't accept failure, if you don't encourage risk, it is unlikely that you're going to get great innovation."

An old virtue, patience, counter-intuitively helps important innovations mature as markets and new technologies evolve ever faster. "Patience is needed as well when it comes to innovation," notes Olli-Pekka Kallasvuo. "This is very, very, very difficult very often." Every CEO has his or her own methods to manage the frustration and tension that patience must calm, for the gestation time of major innovations can be considerable. For example, Bosch devoted 15 years to introducing the Electronic Stability Program braking technology. The company took 20 years to perfect a high-performance diesel direct injection system.

Synchronizing innovation and business strategies is a major CEO responsibility, as Cescau observes:

because innovation is central to strategy and strategy is basically my domain and that of the top leadership team, it is on my agenda in many ways …. I set the standard for the performance of the company, the stretch, the contribution that innovation should make.

At SAP, the CEO along with the board defines the innovative stretch the software company intends to pursue over the next four to six years. "What you do as a CEO in our company is first of all you start normally from a strategic point of view," says Henning Kagermann, then "… you start making strategic assumptions, direction, also around product innovation in our case …. Now you have a very big frame you cannot escape."

Strategic risk has increased considerably because of multiple factors familiar to executives, such as greater complexity, more and new competitors, larger, more fluid markets and faster product cycles. Managing risks has always defined CEO leadership, but the difficulty today is that many historical risk management profiles and formulas are outdated.

"The vital need for speed in almost every aspect of business is paramount today," says George Buckley. "How do you innovate faster, how do you create faster? The answer is you've got to take more risks. So risk management and the acceptance of risk is an incredibly important element of growth and faster innovation." Fujio Cho confirms that competitive pressures have greatly increased the need for speed, complicating risk assessment. "Under such intense conditions, it is impossible to settle down, relax, and concentrate without haste on finding a solution. We are forced to think while we're running. This situation in itself is a challenge that we have to face."

Innovation is another expression for change and many people find it difficult to accept, let alone anticipate, change. To manage this understandable tendency, the CEO should apply diplomatic and motivational skills by acting as the company's principal change agent. To help the organization adapt, Kallasvuo advocates incremental, proactive changes. Dismissing the notion that "if it ain't broke, don't fix it" as a prescription for complacency, he recommends "challenging and questioning" the current paradigm, never a simple matter for large organizations:

> You need to fix things before they get broken in business. In that way, you evolve taking baby steps all the time. From a mindset point of view that's always difficult, and this relates very much to innovation because organizations tend to say, "Hey, why the change? This works." Then you have to say, "but we need to change proactively before things get broken, and in that way evolve." And very often in business, if you have to make a really big change, you have typically failed to make small changes often enough. In that way I believe very much in evolution, as opposed to revolution in making things happen.

Familiarity breeds creativity, and the more conversant a CEO and senior management are with their products, services, and customers, the more likely the CEO will guide the company into promising areas for innovation. "I think if you're not innovative, you should look at the processes, how is information shared, how is the collaboration? Are people telling you what you want to hear, versus absolute adherence to facts?" observes Jim Balsillie. "When you create that kind of realness to it, all the natural, powerful and beneficial forces take over."

The CEO should look to demonstrate a commitment to

innovation in many ways, and some of the most effective are by simply visiting R&D laboratories, departments, and research centers, as well as reviewing prototypes. "Another important function of the CEO is to regularly visit the R&D sites and talk to people working in the R&D area," advises Fujio Cho. Buckley, a vocal advocate of innovation, remarks, "I probably spend 5 to 10 percent of my time on innovation ... talking to the engineers, talking to the scientists, talking about process, talking about products, talking about scientific breakthroughs, talking about prioritization."

As previously mentioned, the CEO should define the standards and expectations for innovative performance. Mirroring the pattern of successful inventions where 1 percent inspiration and 99 percent perspiration yield success, defining innovation policies and priorities is only the start. Success comes from when the CEO repeats the innovation message to the organization. Fehrenbach underscores the essential need for consistency: "Seeking new solutions day by day demands a lot of consistency, and consistency demands strong convictions. Admittedly, cultivating such convictions in a large, international, and highly diversified company is sometimes far from easy." Hence, the importance of CEO role modeling to deliver the innovation message. As Cescau advises:

> he or she needs to show to the organization that innovation is important, that he's really the champion. Because if the CEO is not role modeling, if people don't take their cues from their leader, and if the CEO doesn't seem passionate about the brand, about innovation, about growth, then it is not going to be important for the organization.

2. Celebrate an innovation culture

One of the most mysterious aspects of any company is how a culture originates, evolves, and blossoms over time; how corporate values act as both seed and fertilizer. All CEOs express unanimity about genuinely enlisting and promoting innovation as a key value to advance the company's purpose and mission. Senior management should treat innovation not as a serendipitous activity, but as a corporate trait to be fostered by the proper mindset. The company's values and mission statement are the most visible indication. "Of our four core values at Nokia," notes Kallasvuo, "one is a Passion for Innovation. That's very much highlighted in communications with employees, we discuss the values frequently with our people. In that way we live our dreams under that value, a Passion for Innovation."

For most of its more than 120-year history, Bosch's prodigious output of innovative products appeared without the guidance of published values or a mission statement. In the late 1990s as the company employed increasing numbers of non-Germans, senior management felt the need to codify the corporate values imparted by its founder and successfully transferred through several management generations. These values are encapsulated in a pithy mission statement: "BeQIK, be better, be Bosch." "Be" stands for operating result (*Betriebsergebnis*), "Q" represents quality, "I" stands for innovation, "K" indicates *Kundenorientierung*, customer orientation, all of which concisely describe the attributes of innovative companies.

The CEOs endorse similar views about other values that contribute to innovative performance: high-quality standards, discipline, and independent thinking. High-quality standards are an innovation soul mate because innovations in manufacturing, service techniques, or product functions are often required to improve quality. "Quality affects everything we do," observes Kallasvuo. "Improving quality means doing things better and you need innovation in order to keep being able to do things better."

While discipline and hard work are obviously fundamental to gaining superior results, starting from and reviewing basic first principles is sometimes overlooked, perhaps because it could challenge established methods. The independent thinking that flows from examining first principles can yield highly innovative results. "So innovation is just thinking first principles for everything." advises Balsillie. "How you organize a company, how we reward people, how we track people, how we build the culture, how we partner, how we go to market .... It's all first principles for us." Conventional wisdom is another term for secondhand thinking, an approach rejected at Genentech:

> We certainly have been successful, in part, because we never accept the status quo, we never accept conventional thinking, conventional wisdom. When you look at the points in the history of our company where we have made the biggest difference, in almost every case it was where everybody, almost all the experts, thought that we were doing something stupid.

"Our aspirations are our possibilities" has brightened prospects at Infosys, and all the CEOs endorse bold ambitions. The urges to "leapfrog" the competition, and "kick off the next wave," are expressions of seeking breakthroughs in technologies, business models, and services. But while challenging current paradigms stirs the imagination, cold realistic analysis turns dreams into market success. Ironically, although corporations around the world spend billions annually on market research, they sometimes overlook a free tool to interpret data: unbiased, rational thinking. A sofa-long list of psychological obstacles, including wishful thinking, prejudices, and historical blocks, can cloud clear analysis. Citing the reasons for RIM's Blackberry success, Balsillie remarked:

> I would say the first key reason is we were governed by the facts. There can be a lot of hype and distortion in technology and telecom, but at the end of the day the facts of physics and the facts of economics don't lie. So really having the rigor and the commitment to the analytics are the core drivers.

Correctly interpreting market signals introduces one of the most difficult aspects of reality-based perspectives for both companies and individuals––embracing the flexibility and courage to change, especially during successful times. Complacency is a well-known ailment of many large companies, and overcoming an organization's conservative tendencies is a constant challenge. "You have to breed a culture that says it's acceptable to throw away old things in order to move forward with your dream," suggests Buckley. The widely shared remedy is for the CEO to be the chief change agent directing a policy of continuous incremental change.

While executives are very familiar with the high cost of R&D, several CEOs emphasize the critical importance of continuity in spending levels. "There is nothing worse than when innovation teams are just on the roll and have to stop because there are not enough funds," comments Fehrenbach. "This really destroys the creative flow." As might be expected, the temptation to reduce R&D expenditures during a recession should be resisted, although resource allocations may need to be adapted to advance more promising short-term innovation candidates. But cycles change and the company should prepare for the upswing.

"I think companies need to resist two great temptations: first, when times are good the temptation is to add investment and costs that are not necessary, fat if you like; and, second, when times are bad, the temptation is to stop R&D," advises Buckley.

Recruiting and retaining highly skilled, capable staff and providing excellent equipment are obviously essential to achieving superior innovative performance. Perhaps less self-evident is job rotation to keep personnel stimulated by new challenges, and opening the organization to new stimuli in the quest for innovation.

An innovation-friendly environment, whose qualities will largely depend upon the company's culture and mission, is of course important. Working conditions, administrative procedures, company events, all these and more help create a supportive environment for innovation if senior management deems them important.

3. Engage more innovation partners by sharing knowledge

If any more confirmation was needed to show how demanding world markets have become, the widespread admission by large innovative companies that they can't do it all themselves should settle the issue. "There is so much knowledge and skills in the company that it is easy to start thinking we do have enough," Kallasvuo notes, "although we don't have enough in terms of skills and capabilities."

Buckley recounts, "3M traditionally would invent just about anything and everything it wanted or needed ... slowly we've begun to look more outward."

Companies pursue multiple approaches to access external innovative talent and expertise. These include building relationships with select academic institutions, establishing a presence at technology clusters, acquiring innovative companies and technologies, investing venture capital, expanding corporate partnerships including those with competitors, and forming open innovation networks.

Before briefly noting some of these ways to find innovative partners, it is important to acknowledge signs of a more relaxed approach to intellectual property, which embraces the adage, "you have to give to receive." Kagermann explains, "We have learned that sharing knowledge is the best way to get knowledge. If you feel you have to protect yourself, you have already lost half of the game. The point is to be faster than the others through openness and sharing." SAP protects itself with a few large joint-development partners, such as Microsoft and IBM, but 90 percent of the time extends an open door.

Genentech, in contrast to the secrecy generally practiced in the pharmaceutical industry, enthusiastically publishes discoveries and inventions at an early date, relying on the patent system for necessary IP protection. This open policy engenders professional relationships with leading academics who may participate in joint research projects, and more broadly, helps advance the biotech field and the market.

Steel, concrete, and glass are also strengthening casual relationships with academia as companies endow research buildings at universities and establish neighboring research outposts. Nokia and Bosch, for example, recently inaugurated research facilities in Palo Alto, because notwithstanding the

Internet's ability to transfer knowledge, they find no substitute for physical proximity to inspire fruitful conversations.

Previous inhibitions against making acquisitions, such as at SAP and Nokia, which had historically relied on strong organic growth, are being relaxed to access innovative resources or promising markets. A major incentive is speed. 3M, for example, recently purchased a company founded by a Russian mathematician who had invented an efficient video method to simplify casting tooth impressions for orthodontists. Buckley estimated 3M could have designed a similar technology in five to seven years, "but we would have had to build development teams, taken lots of time, and spend a great deal of money doing it. So what we bought in this case was speed."

The pressure to anticipate rapidly changing technology cycles stimulates the formation of partnerships to exploit emerging technologies and market opportunities. At Unilever, partnering is "essential; it's not important, it's essential," notes Cescau. At Nokia, a Corporate Alliances Board run by a senior executive is in place to "make sure that we have enough focus on partnering, because partnering is so important when it comes to innovation."

In some cases, the trend extends to partnering with competitors. Such partnerships have long been endemic in high technology, but they are relatively recent in other sectors. However, major global challenges such as climate change, energy, and resource sustainability are so pervasive and complex that partnering with competitors on basic research offers efficiencies, as well as the potential for future independent applied research. As Fehrenbach observes:

I mentioned our commitment to continuous improvement. This commitment means we are constantly changing. In the future, more of our work will be done in research networks with other companies. In the past, Bosch generally tried to develop everything on its own or in joint projects with our customers. But we have not worked very often with other companies, or with competitors. Now that we are faced with such enormous challenges as climate change or the need for energy, I believe that we will be working more and more in research networks together with other companies. Such challenges require a concerted effort.

Open innovation is a hot concept today, and in the battle for consumers, new open innovation networks promise to speed R&D development paths, improve quality, and reduce costs. At Unilever, to gain this winning combination, the company must first build the technology platforms and train managers with the skills to orchestrate network of upwards of 40 different entities. As Cescau describes this new direction:

> The job of the science today for me is as much about defining the network and being in control of the network. There's going to be stuff in it which we will do ourselves, because that's where we will derive our competitive advantage. For the rest, we take it from the best. And we do that in advertising, we do that in communication, we do that in the way we run our business, and we should do that exactly the same in science.

4. Organize diversity to promote positive friction and cross-fertilization

Multinationals, with their wide range of products, personnel, services, and markets, are on the front lines facing cultural diversity. A company's skill in managing this diversity goes a long way toward defining innovative performance. "Diversity is really a key word when it comes to innovation in my mind," observes Kallasvuo. "And the positive friction you get from diversity is extremely important. Teams that don't have diversity innovate less in my opinion."

Integrating personnel of different nationalities and backgrounds into cohesive teams can be challenging, especially at companies that historically employed a relatively homogeneous workforce. Recognizing the importance of diversity, Bosch recently elevated cultural diversity to a corporate value and introduced programs to encourage transnational understanding. Fehrenbach comments:

> I think you also have to learn cultural change. One of our values is cultural diversity. We have to be open to this if we want to be really successful and grow internationally. After all, our future growth will be in the emerging markets. We devote a lot of effort to cultural training before we send Germans on assignments outside the country, and before non-Germans come to us.

Mutual respect helps orchestrate well-functioning, culturally diverse teams, and Nokia has extended the concept of respect to treat all Nokia companies equally. The term "off-shore" is considered irrelevant because Nokia wants to encourage a sense of genuine partnership and shared responsibility among the Nokia family of companies. As Kallasvuo explains:

> If you are a global company and you have operations everywhere, the whole concept of off-shoring becomes

irrelevant. For us there is no such thing. I have been talking about this to some US companies who are using the term. You are making a mistake if you look at it in this way. There is no off-shoring, you're just present in different places.

He mentions India to illustrate how mutual respect works in practice:

We have put the head office of a global unit in India, the services unit within Nokia Siemens Networks. So the guy who's running that has global responsibility for that business, but the unit is based in India. This is extremely energizing to the teams in India because they see they are an equal part of the total, as opposed to subordinated in some way. It's very, very important.

The drive to create a "one team" mentality extends to coordinating R&D centers of excellence across research areas, and aligning R&D with business strategy and business models. A free flow of information and investigations among different R&D centers has been a hallmark of 3M. Not only do all employees own the company's intellectual property, there is no prejudice or inhibition against "borrowing" technology developed in one area and applying it in another. Techniques designed for combining chemicals in dentistry, for example, have been applied to improve mixing catalysts for car body repair.

Like travel, exposure to expertise, developments, and processes in different corporate areas can stimulate new ideas, applications, and innovations. Bosch is the largest manufacturer of micro-mechanical sensors (MEMS), and Bosch licenses its MEMS chip process to chip factories around the world. Bosch's original products were for the automotive sector where generations are three to six years. For strategic reasons, in the 1920s the company diversified into consumer goods, but the new product lines also yielded manufacturing process and design benefits for its automotive division, because generation times in consumer goods are much shorter, sometimes as quick as five months. The skills and techniques to speed development of MEMS applications for consumer products, for example, have in turn stimulated process innovations for the automobile sector.

5. Use customer needs to drive simultaneous R&D and business model innovation

Tapping into customer needs is a well-known fount of innovation. At Unilever's Ben & Jerry's ice cream, customers submit, on average, 5,000 ideas for new products every quarter! RIM's Blackberry network now comprises over 130,000 servers, and "for product innovation," says Balsillie, "much of it comes from customer collaboration. We have a structural feedback loop." In the intensely competitive automotive markets, Toyota finds that rather than explore new ideas from the "seed" level, they do better to concentrate on satisfying existing customer needs. "I believe I am not mistaken saying," observes Cho, "that innovation based on needs is faster, cheaper and a more dependable approach." Infosys sends key research lab personnel to meet with customers, because "unless our researchers realize what the outside world is and what is happening in the trenches, their innovations will have no value for the customer."

Listening to customers to gain a better understanding of market realities and trends is not only a matter of having an open ear. An open mind to new possibilities, as Kagermann advises, is also recommended:

> Two things are key to product innovation: One is to listen to the customer, and the second is not to listen to the customer. If you only listen to the customer, you will never make the really good stuff. If you never listen to the customer, you may not survive. So, you have to listen and select between what's really needed and what customers just believe they need.

Coordinating innovation and business strategies has become critical to reduce risk and enter promising markets. Beyond such prudent measures as balancing incremental and breakthrough innovations, and planning successive technology generations, several CEOs refer to the stimulating challenge of engaging R&D teams in business model design. Once considered the turf of senior management, business modeling has entered the R&D arena because digitization, the Internet, and new markets and distribution channels offer a sometimes bewildering array of business options to influence development paths.

Coordinating R&D priorities and business models will require some scientific and engineering personnel to gain business skills. Kallasvuo notes changes in priorities and attitudes at the Nokia Research Center, whose mission today includes business model design:

> We have now assigned them responsibility also to innovate business models and how technologies and business models link, and have an impact on each other. I think this has been very energizing for that team of people who previously have been looking just at technologies. Now

they are seeing the business model at the same time as they are making technology innovation. That has been a very, very positive experience.

Unilever has been changing the R&D brief to take better advantage of the company's far-flung and historical reach in developed and emerging markets. "I'm more and more convinced that R&D, as well as brand development," observes Cescau, "are going to be more and more linked and interacting together." Unilever is overhauling its worldwide network of research centers and smaller innovation centers to create more flexible structures to share expertise and consumer insights across departments and markets, as well as tap into expert resources outside the company. This new open-innovation network, more holistic in scope and flexible than traditional in-house research, portends the future.

6. Set high-quality standards and demanding challenges

High-quality standards spur innovation, but also tempt a pursuit for perfection. Several CEOs warn that the object of R&D, as all areas of business, is optimization, not perfection. Deadlines, set in line with the project's priorities, as well as the need for patience, can help transform innovations into products, as Buckley explains:

> So the looming danger at this stage [prototype] is the tendency to over invent, over perfect and over design. I know all about this because I used to do it myself. Without the discipline of market demands, you're tempted to keep inventing from now all the way to Armageddon. You've got to impress on your people when "time's up!"

and when it's time to stop inventing and start producing.

Setting demanding innovation challenges to realize high dreams inspires individuals and teams to perform their best. Ideally, these goals are viewed as worthy tests of ability, stimulating professional pride. Genentech, for example, has over the years delivered a series of powerful new drugs and medicines, in part by hiring and motivating exceptionally well-qualified scientists and clinicians. "The best people want the opportunity to do the groundbreaking research," notes Levinson. "They don't want to be simply told, look here's a target, make 8,000 molecular derivatives of this starting chemical and see which one binds the tightest. That's nice and really important, but you tend not to have the smartest people getting excited about doing only that." Job rotation is a similar technique to stimulate staff by setting new challenges.

Correctly evaluating R&D progress and rollouts has important implications beyond any particular initiative. If innovations are not properly measured and assessed, promising R&D efforts could be aborted prematurely, immature products could go to market, or future R&D programs could suffer by repeating improper procedures or not replicating best practices.

The risks of using inappropriate measures to review innovative research and development are illustrated at 3M, where George Buckley's predecessor had applied Six Sigma rules to R&D. While Six Sigma can significantly improve continuous repeatable manufacturing, the metrics are inappropriate to innovation, which is not a repeatable process. When Buckley was appointed CEO, he found that:

after we had gone down the Six Sigma pathway for about five years many of our R&D people felt they were being blamed for slowing the pace of innovation .... And that time period was characterized by excessive use of dashboards and measurements, and the application of Six Sigma all across the company, including in the R&D function ... but invention and creativity is a fundamentally discontinuous process. Once you clamp that creativity off, by inserting too much control, no matter how well-meaning it is, there are all manner of unintended consequences: disillusionment, turnover, early retirements and malaise, like a fly wheel running down.

To help spin the fly wheel up, he eliminated Six Sigma rules for R&D, and innovative performance responded favorably.

Infosys assesses software and consulting innovations by revenue, because innovations are judged to have no value unless they produce greater turnover or profits than current techniques. Politically neutral revenue-based evaluations also promote an innovation-based meritocratic culture. As Murthy comments:

All decisions will have to be taken based on data. There should not be any histories of bias from prior transactions in the current transaction. That is, we have to start every transaction on a zero base so that youngsters are confident of winning the current transaction even though they lost the previous transaction. That is why we, at Infosys, celebrate the adage, "in God we trust, everybody else brings data to the table."

In the highly competitive consumer products industry, single samples of products that failed to catch the consumer's eye could stock warehouses. Cescau remarks that reviewing the performance of launch and marketing plans is therefore as important as analyzing the innovative product's development cycle:

> For each innovation we have a set of key performance indicators that we are following when the innovation is launched. Comparing these with the launch objectives, we determine what is going right and what is going wrong and what should be corrected. So it's a very disciplined system where we track in market performance from a product performance, an attitude performance and a business performance, and take action.

Holistic reviews can also point to many areas outside products that often require innovation, such as marketing, finance, and after-sale services. "One needs to remember," says Kallasvuo, "that innovation does not happen in technology alone. It happens in all areas of business. We invest a lot of money on marketing, adding a lot of value in marketing the brand. Innovation happens there as well .... Business model innovation is becoming more and more important."

[*Editors' note: The following drivers, while important, were cited less frequently in the interviews.*]

7. Encourage youth and keep a challenger mentality

Every parent knows young people can bubble with ideas and enthusiasm, and guiding these energies in positive directions sometimes seems a daunting and perpetual task. But the rewards to a parent seeing a child move successfully into new and perhaps unexpected areas also accrue to companies that can find ways to harness youthful talent. Infosys makes a point of engaging young people in the race to develop new software and improve existing routines. "We have to encourage youth," advises Murthy, "because youth is all about new ideas ... we have to create an environment where the young people, are very confident, they are very energetic and they are very enthusiastic to add value to the corporation." Not only does the company's meritocratic culture applaud professional brilliance, Infosys reserves up to three days for a generously defined "Innovation Day" where only people under 30 can present ideas and suggestions to senior management. This practice gives young people respect and exposure to their ideas, and confirms that Infosys genuinely wants to encourage innovation from even the most junior staff.

Closely related to youthful enthusiasm are a challenger's energy and drive, seeking to unseat the incumbent. However, should the challenger succeed, the spoils of victory may fade unless the company shows continuing stamina for risk taking and focus. Kallasvuo, reflecting on Nokia's dominant global market position, observes:

> Although we are now an incumbent, for a long time we were a challenger, a small company attacking the incumbents. I think the challenger mentality continues to be very much here at Nokia. We do understand that when you are a challenger you have to go for it, as opposed to defend. And that challenger culture, freedom to fail, so to speak, is there very much in the company .... A small company soul in a big corporate body, I think is a very important aspect, and that's something we try to nurture and maintain very much.

"You've got to be enthused by being able to reinvent your own future," recommends Buckley. A mindset delighting in constant innovation is highly desirable, but human nature being what it is, success can dim the urge to reinvent. "People understand the need for urgency easily during recession," explains Murthy. "The bigger challenge you have is creating a sense of urgency for innovation where things are going well and when sales are rising rapidly." Infosys applies a policy of planned obsolescence to keep staff focused on innovation. For example, the company developed a versatile platform, *Influx*, to design high-performance software systems with advanced architecture, design, and performance engineering models. After a couple years when Infosys benefited exclusively from these capabilities, the company gave *Influx* to customers. By so doing, it gave Infosys software engineers a new competitive challenge: to improve *Influx*'s performance for the next software development cycle.

8. Appoint appropriate decision makers and encourage transparent information sharing

Assigning informed decision makers at each stage of the R&D review process is critical. Because beauty is in the eye of the beholder, some companies may confuse authority with expertise. Levinson recounts instances in the pharmaceutical industry where executives without sufficient scientific knowledge determine the fate of research initiatives, and questions whether this is beneficial for either the quality of the decisions or R&D staff morale. The standards and criteria for advancing R&D projects should similarly be appropriate and well understood, balancing realistic performance expectations with the need for the creative freedom so essential for inventing and pursuing innovations.

Transparency, among its many benefits, advances innovation because accuracy and networking help the organization to spot and assess opportunities, correct faults, and improve performance. Some well-known types of information sharing are innovation fairs, best practice sharing forums, workshops, and company conferences with industry and academic guests. Companies are also discovering new ways in which the Internet improves access to information. Nokia, for example, initially explored wikis as a collaboration medium in 2004, and today the Nokia intranet hosts over 1,000 wikis. Transparency also helps prevent potential CEO isolation. As Jim Balsillie advises, "When you're highly interrelated with the customers, and you're highly interrelated with the channel, and you're highly interrelated with the partners, and you have close collaboration in different forms of the company, the imperatives naturally come out."

9. Use processes judiciously

If one area might promise to be a "magic bullet" candidate for innovation, the most likely would be processes that control how innovations evolve. Although poor processes certainly retard innovation, there are no guarantees that "ideal" processes will generate predictable results. Luck and serendipity play too much of a role. Art Levinson notes after almost three decades at one of the few successful biotech companies:

I think a lot of it has to do with randomness. I think a culture can squash innovation, but you can't start with a bunch of people and say, all right, we're going to do A, B, C, D, and E, and wonderful things will necessarily come out of that. The best thing you can do, at least in part, is to make sure that you eliminate obstacles to creativity and innovation. We try to do that at Genentech.

George Buckley strongly agrees: "you can organize for innovation, you cannot make creativity a process .... If you could reduce invention and innovation to a process, and if everybody can therefore learn it, the best you can ever hope to be is average."

Notwithstanding the whims of "lady luck" or the difficulty of "legislating" for innovation, a significant consensus among the CEOs suggests that processes can be designed to remove obstacles and create favorable conditions. "I think the key thing that I've learned on innovation," reflects Balsillie, "is that innovation lies much more in process than just having the right answers. So there's a real premium on visibility, in transparency, in collaboration, and I think that goes a tremendous way." Kagermann observes, "I speak a lot about processes and organization to come to scale, speak less about invention. The reason is that I believe this is still the bigger piece of the challenge." Cescau notes:

> We are very clear about our innovation process, and we are also very disciplined in our process. This requires leadership, especially at the start of new projects. We have a uniform innovation process used throughout the company, which is about ideas, feasibility, capability, and rollout. Projects move from gate to gate, requiring a green light at each check point to move on. We also exert a lot of senior management judgment to assess individual

projects at each gate. We don't let a thousand flowers bloom; we prune as necessary.

Company processes differ according to business customs and culture, but they share several common principles. Great emphasis is placed on collegial teams, preferably culturally diverse, working in a collaborative open environment. "First of all," advises N. R. Narayana Murthy, "we have to create an environment of openness where any idea coming from anybody, irrespective of the hierarchy, can be discussed, debated, and accepted." Visibility and transparency in decision making are also vital, particularly with regard to rigorously analyzing opportunities and results.

10. Incentivize to innovate continuously

There is relatively little agreement on the nature and qualities of incentives, aside from the universally recognized need for incentives to encourage continuous innovation. Substantial variations on how individuals should be rewarded financially suggest that personal financial gain is not a prime motivator; if this were not so, we might expect to see more uniformity across innovation incentive packages. While there is a general pattern to reward team performance, rather than individuals, some companies are quite liberal in compensating individual achievements.

Genentech grants substantial stock options, as well as other forms of enhanced monetary compensation, to strong performers. "I'm a big fan of rewarding people who have made really important contributions," says Levinson. "... And, again, that's different from most other companies in the pharmaceutical industry, where in general, the stock options go to a small handful of people." The company recognizes the contribution of less prominent employees by offering almost all employees stock options, which is another policy contrary to standard pharmaceutical industry practice. Bosch rewards individuals according to a tiered incentive formula, depending whether an innovation applies to a manufacturing process or results in a patent.

SAP earned its reputation by integrating software, and the company structures financial innovation incentives in a similar fashion. Individuals are compensated primarily by team performance, and senior executives are rewarded by how well their teams contribute to overall company results. "We always believe it's not one person," remarks Kagermann, "it's more a team that leads to success."

At Infosys, where margins depend upon efficiently reusing existing software code for successive clients, the company developed simultaneously a knowledge bank to store code and a business model of financial incentives to encourage employees to "deposit" code for reuse. When code is "withdrawn" from the bank by other employees, the author earns Knowledge Currency Units commensurate with the level of reuse. At the end of the year, accumulated units can be exchanged for cash or other forms of reward. After more than a decade, the extremely popular bank has become an Infosys institution, and is considered a major contributor to the firm's efficiency.

Symbolic incentives and emotional rewards, such as banquets and special awards to honor high performers, are also in the basket of incentives. Several CEOs point out that a powerful incentive is simply seeing customers use a product or service: "there is no higher reward for an engineer or scientist than to see their products in production and lauded by our customers," says Buckley. Balsillie agrees:

an absolutely supercritical part of the innovation cycle is that engineers want to see their work adopted in the marketplace. At the end of the day, they get their charge out of seeing their stuff used. That's a validation of what they bring to the world. Having market success is an incredible feedback loop to the innovation cycle.

INNOVATION BARRIERS

As might be expected at highly successful, innovative companies, the leading real-time concerns are execution constraints, finding enough skilled personnel or appropriate partners to proceed with expansion plans. Innovation barriers were viewed more in terms of watch-outs, areas to monitor, rather than problems needing solutions. Nonetheless, the CEOs identified several potential innovation barriers.

Execution constraints

Enjoying an abundance of ideas, setting priorities, and assigning appropriate resources are the central concerns for the interviewee companies. "We have always more ideas and opportunities than we can actually deliver to the market," notes Kagermann. "So we have to educate our people that it's not about having even more ideas, but about picking the right ones and bringing them to the customer as part of an optimized portfolio." Execution pressures can be intense. RIM seeks to double engineering headcount in a year. Unilever has pursued a policy of winnowing projects, and over the past couple of years has reduced projects by five to one so the organization can execute more substantial initiatives that "avoid all the clutter." Planning and resource allocation requirements make execution an ever more critical issue for successful innovations. "Do you realize," Cescau asks, "that, theoretically, in quarter one 2008, we should be talking about our 2010 innovation plans with our customers, staff, and in some cases co-creating with them?" This explains why he views "capability to execute" as a major concern.

Managing transition to production

Product or service innovations may improve performance, capabilities, or add value for the customer, but an innovation is only recognized as an innovation when it enters the marketplace. The many steps to take a product through the manufacturing process, pass quality controls and market tests, and move to distribution obviously depend upon the nature of the industry or service. Buckley observes:

> But the dilemma that any really creative company faces is, you start off with something which is basically disorderly, the invention stage, and eventually you have to transition it to something which is highly disciplined, that is, manufacturing. And managing this thing which is initially creative entropy and getting it then to absolute predictability in a smooth transition is an interesting challenge for many companies.

Quality control has always been a key element in this transition process. Today, rapid cycles raise the costs and risks for deficient quality control procedures because they can either delay a product's launch, or worse, damage a brand's reputation. At SAP, where the software's quality has been a major selling point, the company's reputation complicates real-time tests with customers. "So we have the advantage of a good brand name, but this can become a disadvantage if our logo is on a solution that does not completely meet our standards," says Kagermann. "In many cases, testing our market with a quick solution is not possible." These types of quality control issues are likely to become more prevalent as speed to market becomes more important across a wide range of fast-changing competitive technologies.

Bureaucracy and vested interests

Successful innovations are like salmon struggling upriver to spawn. The determined fish encounter patches of smooth water broken by rapids. If the season brings treacherous rapids, or the fish lack stamina or strength, they may flounder before spawning. Bureaucracy can sometimes resemble rapids. Most companies are aware of the risks of excessive administrative layers and procedures, but Levinson counsels that smoothing administrative rapids by itself won't spawn innovation:

> So we've worked hard to keep things simple. But keeping things simple doesn't necessarily mean that you're going to do wonderful things. It means that if things are extremely complicated and slow and bureaucratic, and if someone does have a good idea, you're likely to miss it. I think part of this is making sure that you do things that don't get in the way of people.

A common bureaucratic barrier is vested interests defending resource allocations. At Infosys, the first innovation challenge is to innovate constantly, and Murthy identifies the second as preventing large, established revenue producers from inhibiting new prospects. "As the organization becomes larger and larger, and as we focus on bigger and bigger initiatives, the smaller innovations get brushed away by the powerful forces in the organization which bring huge revenues through well-proven innovations." Infosys ties financial incentives to new innovative initiatives to remind senior executives on not "killing small, innovative ideas, which will, perhaps, become huge revenue earners tomorrow."

Complacency

The perils of incumbency and complacency are often cited, but the high rate of prominent corporations that drop off the stock exchanges suggests the warnings can be poorly applied. In many cases they were never heeded because the company believed it owned a special franchise, such as protected markets, product lines, or customer loyalty that gave immunity from competition.

The CEOs repeat in different words the importance of fighting complacency, such as constantly changing in small incremental steps, challenging the status quo, or imagining bold new futures. One of the most powerful antidotes to complacency is keeping the organization close to the ground, in touch with customers and changing markets; in other words, reality. As Kallasvuo advises:

external orientation is so important when it comes to innovation. Big companies so easily become internally driven. And very often when you get internally focused, you lack the diversity as well, which is so important because that positive friction, like I said, is extremely important.

Inconsistent R&D financing

"You have to spend money to make money" is an old adage that partly applies to innovation. The missing element is the need to spend consistently. Pressures on senior management to reduce funding during a recession, financial stress, or periods of impatience should be resisted. "Looking around in the world you can see why companies under perform. They start a lot of new projects and promising innovations, but as soon as a financial crisis threatens they stop everything and return to the products and services they already know. Later on, these companies are no longer competitive," notes Fehrenbach. "Financial backing must be consistent and reliable."

CEO INTERVIEWS

The following pages present in their own words the CEOs' views about innovation. Some of the questions have been edited by the CEO to reflect better the content of their answers. An Afterword summarizes several innovation trends identified in the interviews that are likely to figure prominently in the years ahead, as companies contend with increasing competition, faster product development cycles, and globalization.

INTERVIEW METHODOLOGY

The editors presented the CEOs with a list of broad questions to stimulate an open inquiry into why their companies are innovative. The CEOs could address the subject as they preferred during an hour-long face-to-face interview. The questions were organized around three major areas, and several sample questions are cited below to indicate the general nature of the inquiry:

Global innovation

- What are the major reasons for your company's innovative performance? What innovation policies and practices have you found to be most productive?

- How is your company using its global reach to stimulate and develop innovative products and services?
- What do you see as major innovation challenges for your company, and how does your company intend to overcome them?

Innovation leadership

- What do you see as the CEO's role in developing innovation strategy and managing performance?
- What are recent examples of innovation at your company, and how are they likely to influence strategy and practices over the next five years?
- As more and more CEOs take a leadership role promoting innovation in their organization, what advice can you give them?

Future innovation strategies

- How do you foresee innovations changing your company and sector(s) over the next five years?
- What areas or aspects of your business are likely to see the most changes or need for innovation over the next five years?
- What strategies and practices do you intend to pursue to meet these expectations?

JIM BALSILLIE

CO-CEO

RESEARCH IN MOTION

Research In Motion (RIM) is a leading designer, manufacturer, and marketer of innovative wireless solutions for the global mobile communications market. The BlackBerry line of smartphones provides mobile access to email, phone, text messages, and the Internet. RIM's integrated hardware, software, and services support diverse wireless network standards, and enable other developers and manufacturers to offer their customers wireless data connectivity. Founded in 1984 in Waterloo, Canada, the company introduced the BlackBerry in 1999. Today, there are millions of BlackBerry subscribers.

BIOGRAPHY

Since 1992, Jim Balsillie has been co-CEO at Research In Motion (RIM), maker of the world renowned BlackBerry wireless handheld system. In 2008 he was named one of the top 30 CEOs WorldWide.

In 2002, Mr. Balsillie founded the Centre for International Governance Innovation (CIGI), a world-class global research institute focused on the restructuring of international governance. In 2007, Mr. Balsillie announced the creation of the new Canadian International Council (CIC) of which he is the

Chair. In 2008, he founded the Balsillie School of International Affairs.

Mr. Balsillie is a graduate of the University of Toronto and the Harvard Graduate School of Business. He is a chartered accountant and a fellow of the Ontario Institute of Chartered Accountants. He also holds numerous honourary doctorate degrees.

INTERVIEW

What are the major reasons for RIM's innovative performance?
I would say the first key reason is we were governed by the facts. There can be a lot of hype and distortion in technology and telecom, but at the end of the day the facts of physics and the facts of economics don't lie. So really having the rigor and the commitment to the analytics are the core drivers.

Deep rigor, understanding the technologies, understanding economics, and the way the world functions when these come together, and then doing fundamental analysis and coming to your own conclusions is the absolute key. It's proper bets, and then being highly engaged, very strong management on implementation of your bets. Those are key things that you can't outsource, you can't delegate, those are very essential to the business. And my partner, Mike Lazaridis, is extremely involved in the technology and is a true visionary. We were also very innovative in our go-to-market strategies, our partnering strategies, our financing strategies, as well as our business model and our technology too.

How do you manage your dual CEO roles?
There's a general separation, and even that is considered a bit innovative, I guess. On the technology side, Mike is

40

definitely our CTO. On the sales side, I'm definitely our chief sales officer. On the production side, supply chain, component engineering, Mike's there. In the middle it's strategy, there's a tremendous amount of interrelationship that fuses. And in partner cultivation and key carrier relationships we divvy them up just based on who you deal with. So there's a pretty natural divvying up, but there's also a huge sharing and partnering.

When it comes to product innovation it's very much Mike and it's not so much me. I think that the key thing I've learned about innovation, is that innovation lies much more in process, than just having the right answers. So there's a real premium on visibility, in transparency, in collaboration, and I think that goes a tremendous way. When different functions of the business meet regularly, even if it's just go-to-market update, there's enormous empathy that develops very quickly, which is critical because the enemy of empathy is victimhood and vice versa.

I've found that in virtually every issue, if you give people the same set of facts, given decent cognitive capabilities and a general well-adjusted personality, they'll come to the same set of conclusions. And virtually all differences come from information gaps. So once you have everybody agreeing with the same set of facts and agreeing on the conclusions, the organization gets to where it wants to go. It's really about getting to the right answer and lots of daily and weekly adjustments in strategy, because you're always adjusting to your realities.

Do you apply your global reach to advance innovation?
Sure, we have R&D in different parts of the world, mainly throughout North America and Europe; we also have customer service throughout the world, localization,

market research, staff, employee satisfaction surveys. We're dealing with corporations all over world, people all over the world, carriers all over the world, and application partners all over the world. So we're a convergence platform, we're kind of a crossroads for these things. We're in a unique spot.

Do India and China play an increasingly important role?

China and India are both important markets. Each country has its own structural realities that are very different from the rest of the world, but you can't help but note that they're growing like crazy and there's a massive amount of people, and you have to create unique strategies in that part of the world. But also when we're emerging so much everywhere, and we're sort of gated by execution capacity, there's always an opportunity cost to what you pursue.

How much do you partner and outsource?

We work with a partner for our outsourced manufacturing. Outsourcing other parts of our business wouldn't work well because it's all about efficiency, integration, and synthesis which doesn't compartmentalize very well. It's not like we're an IBM or Microsoft, with 50 different projects, and you can say, here, you do that one. That approach doesn't work well for us at this time.

What about innovation R&D, such as with academia?

We have a fair bit of partnerships. A number of Canadian universities, and some US universities and some European universities, for sure, very much on the engineering side.

Do you partner with competitors?

There's a tremendous amount of partnering in our business. BlackBerry is a convergence platform with devices. There's always contention on the interface level, how much value-add somebody does and how far you go on the value-add, and what rents somebody accrues for their roles. So that's just endemic in tech and telecom. We work with several hardware manufacturers through our BlackBerry Connect and BlackBerry Built In programs. We support Windows Mobile for BlackBerry, we interface to the major email platforms, we interface to large services. We're a convergence platform.

What are limits to the pace of innovation at RIM?

Resourcing. There's so much opportunity. Mobility and convergence I think are, by far, the hottest, most dynamic sector in tech and telecom today. We've grown 100 percent year over year. We've had 70,000 percent internal organic growth over the last 11 years, so there's not a lack of opportunity in our space. There's just a tremendous execution imperative. Our biggest gate is finding the best people, getting them hired, getting them integrated, getting them leading. It's a huge imperative for us, huge imperative for us.

What is the CEO role to advance innovation?

Mike has weekly vision meetings where he has the engineers in and he talks to them about the status, and the key decisions, and the key activities. My role in the innovation process is really the feedback loop, making sure different parts of the organization are interrelating and collaborating. Definitely on the go-to-market side, to ensure that all aspects of product management and program management and channel management and sales and partner management are interrelated, and they're feeding back their issues to the rest of the company. The big role is to manage the key relationships which Mike and I divvy up, some of which we share. Making sure that people understand the objectives that we're trying to achieve, have the resources they want, are functioning in a cohesive way, have all the information they need.

How do you source and develop innovative ideas?

Part of the answers for ideas lies in the process. When you're highly interrelated with the customers, and you're highly interrelated with the channel, and you're highly interrelated with the partners, and you have close collaboration in different forms of the company, the imperatives naturally come out. But for product innovation, much of it comes from customer collaboration. We have a structural feedback loop.

There comes a time when you have to cut off the features development because you've got to release a product and you go into a heavy, heavy, heavy test cycle, and the more you become mission critical, the more the test cycle becomes super critical, because you're right up there with oxygen in things that are important, and so it has to work. People want features and commitments, but it's got to work. As these things get more complex, the risks of the reliability increase. So again, a very, very difficult tension, when do you cut off features, and when do you cut off testing, when do you go to Alpha, when do you go to Beta, when do you go to production? These are huge. You have to draw a line in the sand.

It's not an exercise in perfection, it's an exercise in optimization and multiple trade-offs.

What are your incentives to stimulate innovation?

It's definitely a culture where you celebrate innovation and reward innovators. We have big innovators' banquets, rewards for patents, and recognition of the innovation culture, and definitely lots of compensation things like perks and options and good pay, and having the industry's best tools. The engineers are respected, they're resourced, they're compensated. But also an absolutely supercritical part of the innovation cycle is that engineers want to see their work adopted in the marketplace. At the end of the day, they get their charge out of seeing their stuff used. That's a validation of what they bring to the world. Having market success is an incredible feedback loop to the innovation cycle.

How would you describe RIM's innovation culture?

Aggressive, very smart, very high-performance small teams, very focused on the rigors of their discipline, but understanding that it's an integrated solution so they have to collaborate and synthesize. Mike, my partner and Co-CEO, is an incredibly good synthesizer. Our employees are very, very loyal, there's very low turnover, they are very, very smart, very aggressive technically, pushing the boundaries always. Our culture has a focus on integrating and synthesizing because you're using a system where your focus is optimization and trade-offs. This is an immensely complex dynamic that is structural in our business. Managing the complexity and distilling it is a strategic advantage for us.

How do you view innovation as a concept?

Everything's innovation when it's all original thought. You're not in any way, shape, or form tied to convention. So innovation is just thinking first principles for everything. How you organize a company, how we reward people, how we track people, how we build the culture, how we partner, how we go to market, how we create our products, what we do, where we do it. It's all first principles for us. It's natural, it's organic, it just becomes second nature, really. You don't set out to be innovative for the sake of innovation. You have your core principles and your core objectives, and you're constantly asking yourself, how can I get this done in the best way possible given the time and resource constraints before me and the huge imperative to get it done?

How do you measure results?

You get pretty good feedback loops. Either your products perform well or they don't. People like them or they don't. We have daily reports of activations by each product and net subscribers by carrier, by channel, by application, worldwide. You have a lot of internal use of the product. So when everybody uses a BlackBerry, people are very demanding and willing to comment on what's right and what's not right, and what they like and what they don't like. So a high adoption rate, and internal utilization rate, and very, very good near-term feedback loops, it's unambiguous if a product's selling well or not. Our feedback loop is an advantage to us, it is ideal.

This is not an exercise in perfection, it's an exercise in optimization. People go hard, and they try to do the right thing, and we generally get the most outcomes that there are to get out of a situation.

And if something's quite wrong, it becomes real apparent, real quick. Doesn't become 100 percent apparent immediately, but it becomes much more apparent, much more quickly than just about any other circumstance I can think of. For such a big, distributed global company, we still have that very clear and specific feedback loop.

Do you foresee potential changes in RIM's innovation strategy over the next five years?

I don't see any big changes in how we do what we do. I think we've been so innovative and continue to be innovative, I think the path forward for us is clear. The role we take is really important, it's expanding. The job we do for the partners, and for the customers, and for the carrier channel partners is clear and valuable and not going away. I think we just have a lot more implementation, a lot more execution, more applications, more carrier partners, different air links, more channels, more sophisticated platform classes, scaling, innovative devices by us, but at the core of it all, I don't see tectonic shifts, as far as I can see. It's possible something could happen and we'll adapt to it as soon as we sense it, but I don't sense a major structural thing happening.

What is the time frame in your industry for innovation?

For products, generally a couple of years. We have a pretty good sense what the next couple of years are going to bring. Anyone who pretends in our world they have a real clear sense of beyond that, I don't think they're being really that clear about it, because there's just so much, so many permutations and combinations, that you're just building castles in the sand of scenarios once you get out past a certain period of time. I mean, people have a pretty good idea what's going to play out in the next couple of years right now, but I'd be pretty skeptical if people have much beyond that really baked out, in a reasonable sense of the word. I mean it's possible, but I doubt it.

What are the main challenges in your industry?

The big things are rapid product cycles in innovation. You can be a hero one day, go very quickly thereafter. So it's the acceleration, it's the dynamism, it's the rapid product cycles. A winner can put you on top, but not for that long. If you keep missing it, you can go really down very quickly. So missing those cycles is incredibly painful, and capitalizing on emerging trends, or others missing their cycles, can be very, very beneficial. So I think just the rapid cycles is the structural reality of our business.

What policies with regards to innovation would you pursue in a recession?

I think if you have a long-term opportunity in your sector, then you should be innovating independent of macro economic trends.

We're fortunate that our sectorial trends are so strong, they're stronger than any macro trends. It's kind of like, metaphorically, selling the color TV set back in the black-and-white TV set days of the 1960s. Recession signs come and TV set sales are down 20 percent. Well, color TV sets were 10 percent of TV sets the previous year and they'll be 20 percent the next year, 15 percent. That's 50 percent growth minus 20 percent, so you're getting 40 percent growth instead of 50 percent growth because of the macro. So you're affected by the macro, but the sectorial is much stronger than the macro. When you have a shift in technologies, the sectorial shift is often stronger than the macro economic shift.

But we can't control it, so I don't spend a lot of time thinking about it. In a rapidly emerging space, we just keep going hard because it accrues a perpetuity of opportunities that are so much bigger and that compound off of where you do today. If you can get your product in six months earlier, what does that mean five years down in the compounding? It's big. As Einstein said, the most powerful force in the world is the formula for compounding. A compounded amount three, four years out at 100 percent growth is enormous, so you get going as fast as you can.

Do you have any advice for other CEOs to improve innovative performance?

I would think that the answer lies in visibility and transparency. We run this weekly meeting, all go-to-market teams with a couple of hundred people every Monday morning for an hour and a half. A hundred people will spend a minute saying what they did the previous week and what they're doing this week. If I miss a couple weeks because I've been traveling, it's almost humbling to get back into it. The easiest thing in the world is to sit in the principal's office and have everyone nervous outside waiting, they come in, and tell you what you want to hear and make you feel good. Then you go home and you're in a buffered charade. It feels good, but it's not real. I think reality is very rewarding, but it's also very real. I think if you're not innovative, you should look at the processes, how is information shared, how is the collaboration? Are people telling you what you want to hear, versus absolute adherence to facts? Are you right on the front line with your product, are you right on the front line with your go-to-market teams, do you meet with customers, do you use your products? When you create that kind of realness to it, all the natural, powerful, and beneficial forces take over.

I think the key is to embrace that in every way. And there is a natural tendency in big companies and people who are new to a job, or not comfortable with things, to pull back from that. Nothing like having a great, big office with people all polite to you all the time, lined up, telling you what you want to hear. But are you really doing your job, are you really driving value, moving the company forward? Or is it a charade to indulge you? Again, I would say if you're not getting what you want out of the company, get in all the way.

GEORGE BUCKLEY

CHAIRMAN, PRESIDENT, AND CEO

3M

3M is a diversified technology company operating worldwide across six business segments: industrial and transportation; health care; display and graphics; consumer and office; safety, security, and protection services; and electro and communications. Founded in 1902 at the Lake Superior town of Two Harbors, Minnesota, 3M has expanded significantly over the years from its core strengths of abrasives, industrial tapes, adhesives, and film products. A recognized leader in research and development, 3M today produces thousands of innovative products for dozens of diverse markets. 3M's core strength is applying its more than 40 distinct technology platforms—often in combination—to a wide array of customer needs. 3M currently employs some 75,000 people worldwide and has operations in more than 60 countries.

BIOGRAPHY

George W. Buckley became 3M Chairman, President, and Chief Executive Officer in December, 2005. Prior to 3M, from June 2000, he was Chairman and Chief Executive Officer, Brunswick Corp., having previously served as President of Mercury Marine Group, Brunswick's largest division.

Before joining Brunswick in 1997, he was President of the US Electric Motors Division, and the Automotive and Precision Motors Division at Emerson Electric Co. in St Louis, Mo. He also served as Chief Technology Officer of Emerson's worldwide group of motor, electronic drives, and appliance-related businesses.

Prior to his responsibilities at Emerson, Buckley was Managing Director (President) of the Central Services Division of the British Railways Board in the UK, responsible for the railway's 14 manufacturing plants, R&D, all shared services, and major construction projects.

Mr. Buckley is a Director of the Black & Decker Corporation and Archer Daniels Midland Company, as well as a member of the Singapore Research, Innovation and Enterprise Council (RIEC), helping guide Singapore's efforts to enhance its biomedical sector.

He completed joint study at the Universities of Southampton and Huddersfield in the United Kingdom, where he was awarded a Ph.D. in Engineering. He also holds a B.Sc. in Electrical and Electronic Engineering and an honorary D.Sc. in Engineering from the University of Huddersfield, and an honorary LL.D. from St Thomas University.

INTERVIEW

What are the major reasons for 3M's innovative performance?
3M has sustained its innovative culture for decades, really almost since the company was founded. I think that the early leaders of 3M understood the power of creativity and imagination, and were really quite ahead of their time in realizing that creativity and imagination had to be managed differently than other aspects of a business.

In other functions efficiency is often the primary goal—

that's not the case with innovation and creativity. I say it jokingly, but humor always has an element of truth in it. That is, if you get behind in innovation, and you think you can install a (Six Sigma) process to try to correct, you can't schedule yourself for three good ideas next Wednesday and two on Friday. So while you can organize for innovation, you cannot make creativity a process. It's more about controlling chaos, or at least uncertainty, if not chaos.

If you could reduce invention and innovation to a process, and if everybody can therefore learn it, the best you can ever hope to be is average. So we hope, and I think most people engaged in innovation would hope, that the outcome requires a little bit more than handle turning or process improvement. In fact, the very fact of "improving" a process might well put constraints on people, and may kill the very thing that you hope to achieve.

I think that leaders of 3M over the years have understood and respected the special nature of 3M's culture and have managed the company accordingly. And each generation of 3M has internalized the quest for innovation and worked to keep it alive.

Could you describe the innovation culture at 3M?

The way I describe 3M and the way it works so well, is that it is more like an organism than it is an organization. We have many formal communication processes for our technical people: workshops, sharing of best practices, technology fairs, and the like, and these events happen several times a year. We have technology forums where people share ideas, we talk about market issues, and about what we can do better. For example, can we package ideas in a different way? Can we apply ideas we already have developed in one area in a different area? Do we have nine out of ten pieces of the technology puzzle and we need one more to make a breakthrough here? All those sorts of things get discussed. But the process of innovation at 3M is almost like enzymes being conducted, passed through the body at the cellular level, more like an organism than an organization.

Another element of 3M's culture—which is different than at any company I've ever worked, by the way—is that all the technologies are owned by the corporation. No matter who invests in them or who invents them, all the technologies are common property. We all own them and more importantly, we can all use them in product development. They're communal property.

So for example, I was just recently shown a new automotive body repair product which we make. Some of the new filler materials have very high mixing ratios. When I was repairing cars as a youth with my father, the car body filler and catalyst would maybe have a 10 to 1 or 15 to 1 mixing ratio. They were all mixed by hand, so it was not very accurate and very wasteful of material. New materials and new catalysts have 100 to 1 or more mix ratios, so we use very small amounts of catalyst. So consistent mixing is very difficult to achieve, especially in a production environment. So our folks pondered what to do about this, but didn't ponder very long because of the shared nature of ideas in the company. Within a matter of hours some bright spark realized that we already found the solution in the way we mixed fillers for our dental business. So we applied exactly the same mixing nozzle technology we used in dental technology to an application in car body repair. And you might say, how can this be? This is 3M.

In another example, I was introduced to our paint preparation system (again used mostly in automotive applications) that has special cups and liners that seal the paint gun and hold paint in a replaceable reservoir. These cups and liners replace the familiar aluminum can on the bottom of the spray gun you'd have seen 20 years ago. Less than a month later, I was going around one of the labs (and I love to be in our labs) and I saw exactly the same technology being used on a food pathogen detection project. They'd taken the technology platform that we were using in a paint preparation system and applied it to pathogen detection for food safety. This is the 3M I have come to know and love.

3M has a global reach. You have subsidiaries all around the world and production sites everywhere. Is that an important piece of your innovation strategy?

It becomes a natural evolutionary step for us because we believe very, very strongly in localization. The days when you could invent everything in America and send it to Germany, to Britain, to Japan, to China, they're long gone. They're dead, buried, and the headstone has been firmly set. So, in any major market, we almost always establish a laboratory early. That might not be the first thing we do, but we want to get a lab in place as soon as reasonably possible.

Typically we'll enter a new market and build the business initially through imported products, sometimes through local outsourcing. So we use the lab initially for technical service; helping customers with applications of our products. Then we progressively localize the imported products, depending on the size and scalability of the business. After that, we usually will install local R&D. We divide our R&D spending and activities into five classes. The simplest form of technology support is essentially technical service on an existing product, which is called Class I. So we start there.

As our people go out and provide technical service on these existing products, they always see new things: new applications, customized applications, and the like. We progressively internalize those observations and then we'll move to Class II, Class III, Class IV, and Class V over a period of two, three, four, five years, depending on how the development of the market is progressing and what the local market needs are. Class V R&D is defined as new products in new markets. Over the years, different countries' labs have evolved as centers of excellence for different kinds of technology. But there may be simpler models of that same center of excellence which exist in a number of different nations. So it's not just exclusive in any one location. There is not a one size fits all approach, it's tailored for local market needs.

The United States, for example, has become the center of excellence for surface chemistry and material science. If you go to China, it would be the center of excellence for utility products, in particular medium-voltage cabling accessories such as splices and terminations. In Germany it would be mostly automotive; in France it would be telecoms. Now there are again local derivatives of that in many different markets. Because even in something that you think is as standardized as a telecom splitter, local utilities may or may not approve a particular feature in the base product. So you have to take the general core products and then localize and adapt them.

So it starts simply, but then evolves over time into a more sophisticated R&D approach, steadily moving up to Class IV or Class V as a market grows. And we have such major labs now in Britain, Germany, France, Italy, China, Japan, the United States, Canada, and Korea. And we have emergent smaller labs, new seedlings if you like, in Russia, India, and Dubai. You can well imagine the dispersed nature of the world's business, and we tailor our labs to that fact. Oil and gas extraction is centered in about four different locations in the world, Russia, in the Middle East, Northern

Canada, and the western United States. It doesn't mean that there aren't other places where we sell into the oil and gas market, for there are, in Britain, Norway, where you have offshore applications. Automotive, of course, is fairly broadly dispersed around the world. But overall, that's how the internationalization of our R&D process rolls out.

Do you work a lot with external partners?

Not really. It's probably an area of potential improvement at 3M, and one we are working on right now. 3M traditionally would invent just about anything and everything it wanted or needed. Slowly, and I'm probably being a little bit unfair about this, but slowly we've begun to look more outward. In our core technologies we're always scanning the technical literature, scanning patents, scanning cutting-edge technologies, and if we see an invention coming up that we think advances our core, we're very happy to go out and buy it, if need be. Now obviously, like so many things in life, you're looking for balance, always. You don't want too much internal or too much external sourcing of technology, because too much of one can kill the other if you're not careful, if one or the other gets too strong. So we strive for balance in developing most of the core technologies.

Let me give you an example of a technology transition, in dentistry where we're the second largest manufacturer of dental products in the world. We make bridges, crowns, conformable materials, ceramics; the list is endless. There's about a 40 percent chance if you've got a bridge or crown in your mouth it's made by 3M. In that particular case, if you were taking data for bridges and crowns, and orthodontics—we're the largest manufacturer of orthodontic products in the world—you take a physical model of the teeth, made with an impressioning material, typically it's the blue "goop" most of us have seen. When it's put in the mouth, some people have a gag reflex, so we looked to improve how we extracted the geometric data from the mouth that we need to make a crown. And in addition to the messiness, there are too many steps in the crown production process. So we sought to eliminate some of the steps and make the process more comfortable for customers.

One of my heroes of history, Samuel Johnson, had a lovely saying which I like a lot. He said, "As regards the English language, perfection is not reached when there are no more words to be added, but when there are no more words to be removed." I've adapted his quotation to my business life because it's the same in processes too. "Perfection is not reached when there are no more steps to be added, but when there are no more steps to be removed." And it is true in manufacturing products: "Perfection is not reached when there are no more parts to be added, but when there are no more parts to be removed." So while Johnson was speaking about de-cluttering our language, his wisdom applies in engineering too. I've found that de-cluttering, through a focus on simplicity, always brings with it elegance, reliability, and low cost too.

But let's go back to our dentistry example. You take an impression of the tooth arch with the material, make a cast, then you laser scan the cast, form a digital model, and then feed the data into a multi-axis milling machine that will mill a ceramic block to make your new tooth part, your new bridge, or your new crown. Well, no big surprise, but the data collection method here is antiquated and can some-time provoke a gag reflex in the patient. So we needed a better method of gathering that data, the geometric data we use to machine the crown and avoiding the gag reflex. The answer was always going to be some sort of digital approach. We could probably have developed that technology ourselves in house over time, but who knows how long it would have taken? It might have taken us five, six or seven years. And you only have a small window of time to react when a disruptive technology comes along. And whoever goes through that window first usually wins. Experience and history teaches us that the first two to go through the window usually capture perhaps 80 percent of the marketplace. So you cannot be, you absolutely cannot be the third one through that figurative opening or you're done. Of course, you don't want to be on the "bleeding edge" either.

So we looked at the obvious scanning and data extraction solutions, X-ray, laser, etc., to better gather the data. We then came across a company in Boston led by a Russian mathematician that had a video-based data collection method, so there is no ionizing radiation involved. It was absolutely superb. So we bought the company. Now we could probably have developed that technology inside 3M, but we would have had to build development teams, taken lots of time, and spend a great deal of money doing it. So what we bought in this case was speed.

You might now ask, how does such a thing get integrated into 3M when it's so new, so foreign? Well, it might seem like a "bump on a log" for now, because it's not one of 3M's traditional cores. But I remind you that 3M's first and original core 100 years ago was coated abrasives. It's the only one we had. But today is very different, we have many cores. So many of the things we do today were not core back when. So over time, we integrate, we adopt and we assimilate new technologies that may today be foreign, but within in a few short years become familiar and part of our core. So it's almost like a pac-man strategy where you keep gobbling up and digesting new technologies. That's how we proceed to build an ever-expanding technology core. It's a process of progressive assimilation and adaptation.

Does China or India play a role in R&D?

Increasingly China does, because it's become a center of excellence for electrical products. But it's not the only thing that they do. In fact, what accompanies a center of excellence is replication of other core markets in those new locations. Our people there are brilliant and often come up with some twist on a current product which is better than the original. So of course we backward integrate them, taking them back to their old "home" in revitalized form. It's another form of adaptation and assimilation, a sort of fast evolutionary "natural selection" process if you like. So everybody figuratively "steals" ideas freely from everybody else here in this company. It's marvelous to see how open everyone is to that. You may well have invented something, but everyone is thinking, "I can probably use that on my version of a completely product." There's no loss of face by the new inventor in so doing, and that's another wonderful cultural aspect at 3M. There's no sense of loss of self-worth if somebody else invented something and you're now backing it or using it in your own invention.

I'm not all that familiar with Apple, but a lot of people rightly point to them as an innovative company. They (and Creative Technologies in Singapore before them, who originally developed the digital music player concept) teach us a great example of adaptation. There's nothing fundamentally new in the iPod, all the hardware parts were readily available. It's just the assembly of existing ideas in a different way. It was marketing genius, not engineering genius, that was the breakthrough. They and Creative Technologies identified an unmet consumer need. Where Apple took it a step further was in great industrial design and in the linking of the iPod and iTunes concepts. It was brilliant. And we're no different than that. Where we're very good is where we can bring multiple technologies to bear on a problem, many of which have been used and proven elsewhere. Whereas some companies celebrate a kind of pure play approach, where we are at our best is when it's not a pure play. That's where our business differentiation comes in. And so the breadth of 3M is simultaneously a challenge to manage, and a tremendously powerful competitive weapon. And we try to use it in the best way possible.

What is your role promoting innovation?

At 3M the CEO is genuinely the principal cheerleader of technology. But it's more than that for me, because I also have pet projects ... things I really, really like ... stuff I'm really enamored by and that I promote whenever I can. But my main job is to promote innovation, whether to investors, at a conference; whether it's inside the company or wherever it might be. I make very clear to everyone my absolute and unequivocal support for innovation.

It seems that there was a big change in your approach to innovation compared with that of your predecessor. Was this a difficult change to introduce?

Well, let me give you some context. We needed to change and Six Sigma was the vehicle of choice. But after we had gone down the Six Sigma pathway for about five years many of our R&D people felt they were being blamed for slowing the pace of innovation or that they weren't valued in the "new 3M," whatever that meant. And that time period was characterized by excessive use of dashboards and measurements, and the application of Six Sigma all across the company, including in the R&D function.

Now I understand, and I am philosophically supportive of the classic Deming notion that anything not defined can't be measured, anything not measured can't be controlled, and anything not controlled can't be improved. I fundamentally support that notion.

But with creativity, there has to be a sense of freedom, not anarchy of course, but there has to be a sense of freedom if you want people to invent and be creative. The DMAIC part of Six Sigma is at odds with this because its fundamental objective is to control and to limit.

Six Sigma is intended for use on continuous processes, but invention and creativity is a fundamentally discontinuous process. Once you clamp that creativity off, by inserting too much control, no matter how well-meaning it is, there are all manner of unintended consequences: disillusionment, turnover, early retirements, and malaise, like a fly wheel running down. So my job was to spin the fly wheel back up again. And actually it took a lot less time than I thought.

Now in my own particular case as CEO, I was advantaged by having a Ph.D. in engineering and I had worked in R&D. In fact I started off my career in R&D. So as a young man, I was one of them. And that led to quicker acceptance of me with the technical folks. They said, "OK, this guy has done what we do, he understands how to do it and he understands the benefits and the impediments." So I was given a listening ear, whereas my predecessor, because he was fundamentally a businessman, wasn't. And it may well have been a little bit unfair to him in some ways. But it is what it is. When things don't work, usually both sides are at fault to a degree. R&D folks can sometimes seem like prima donnas, always believing they are right, but it doesn't matter because they are our prima donnas and you have to show them that you love them, which I do. It is fundamentally their talent and genius which makes a company like 3M as good as it is.

How do you help stimulate innovation?

The first thing is the importance of a dream. Now let me explain. Usually the way I explain this is to refer to the movie *South Pacific*. In that movie there's a Balinese lady called Bloody Mary singing on the beach to a group of the American airmen, and she sings a song called "Happy Talk." The words of that song are "Happy talky, talky, happy talk. Talk about things you like to do. You gotta have a dream, if you don't have a dream, how you gonna have a dream come true?"

So you have to start with a dream. And you also have to have an abiding belief that something better can be created than what you have today. Not only must you have a belief that something better can be created, you have to have a willingness to throw the old thing away. We normally call it cannibalization, but remember, if you're an innovator and you make a breakthrough on a product that might last five, ten, fifteen years, you're the person who has to throw that breakthrough away into the trash and say it's not good enough. Innovators have to balance conviction that what they are doing today is right, but also a conviction that what they did yesterday can be bettered. That is a deep psychological and sometimes conflicting burden to carry.

You've got to be enthused by being able to reinvent your own future. And be able to deal with the fact that, yes, I know I designed this pen yesterday, but I can design a better one today, and not be hurt by the fact. You have to breed a culture that says it's acceptable to throw away old things in order to move forward with your dream. But, above all, people need the freedom to dream.

In a sense, innovation and creativity can be almost like a religious quest. There's a great deal of faith involved in the process and inspirational belief enters into the picture—

sometimes belief in things that don't yet exist! As an inventor, you must have this innate belief that you can create things that don't exist and that you are willing to risk a lot personally, in your reputation and effectively in your personal psyche. One success is often accompanied by many earlier failures, and it's tough for people to do sometimes. There's a lovely quotation from George Bernard Shaw who said, "Nothing is worth doing unless the consequences for failure are serious." Psychologically, it can be like that for a researcher who bets on a breakthrough and then the breakthrough doesn't work out or proves to be an illusion. You have to accept that, take it for what its worth, learn from it and move on.

Have you any advice for companies attempting to improve their level of innovation?

I think companies need to resist two great temptations: first, when times are good the temptation is to add investment and costs that are not necessary, fat if you like; and, second, when times are bad, the temptation is to stop R&D. One must avoid the temptation to do either one of those.

So when your product is incredibly successful, when you're getting tremendous growth out of a new product, that's the very time you should be reinventing that product. As they say, "The best time to replace the roof is when the sun is shining." And that is a hard thing for companies to do. And it's hard for people to do as well! If you don't invent a new future for yourself, somebody else will.

The other thing that comes to mind is the concept of a leapfrog, and it's tied to some degree to the earlier Six Sigma discussion. I remember about ten years ago when I was working on a new product at Mercury, I asked these particular product engineers and designers, "Can you make me this product as good as the Japanese can make it?" And they said, well, it'll be about as good; maybe a little bit better in this feature, maybe a little bit worse in that feature. I said, "Wrong answer!" I explained that if you can only make it about as good as your competitors can make it; you'll never do better than the average. I wasn't interested in us being average. So you always have to have a leapfrog strategy in your mind, because that's what's going to help you to surpass the competition. It's also what they will do to you if you don't do it to them first.

So, overall, it's tough to create an environment where dreaming is acceptable and creativity understood. And I think that is one of the struggles inside companies in that people often expect that innovation can be reduced to a process. Now of course, there are some elements that can be part of a process. But the dilemma that any really creative company faces is, you start off with something which is basically disorderly, the invention stage, and eventually you have to transition it to something which is highly disciplined, that is, manufacturing. And managing this thing which is initially creative entropy and getting it then to absolute predictability in a smooth transition is an interesting challenge for many companies.

How do you transition from R&D to manufacturing?

Picture it in three blocks. One block is this somewhat chaotic, somewhat unpredictable sequence of invention and creation of products which we've just spoken about. At 3M we essentially have no process for that; other than input from voice of the customer and best practice sharing forums, so there isn't a definitive way of doing it. Obviously it's driven somewhat by market need and sometimes by seeding technology; sometimes it's technology push and sometimes it's market pull. But even voice of the customer is not enough. I'm reminded here of Henry Ford, who said,

"If I had listened only to my customers, I wouldn't have invented the mass production of cars. What my customers wanted was a faster horse that ate less hay." Voice of the customer (VOC) is a necessary but not sufficient condition for success. There has to be a sprinkle of "magic dust" to produce great products, or whatever it is you wish to call the inspiration that is the mother of invention. Serendipity, accidents, blind luck and other things all play a part. You can't put that into a can or a Six Sigma process.

The second block is once you've actually got a working prototype. And here's where I tell my colleagues, "perfection is the enemy of production." We're not just in business to make bridges and crowns, Post-it notes, high-voltage cabling, and the like. We're in business to make money: that's our primary business! And we do it through the inventive minds of our people and then through the products they produce. So the looming danger at this stage is the tendency to over invent, over perfect, and over design. I know all about this because I used to do it myself. Without the discipline of market demands, you're tempted to keep inventing from now all the way to Armageddon. You've got to impress on your people when "time's up!" and when it's time to stop inventing and start producing. But the saving grace here is that there is no higher reward for an engineer or scientist than to see their products in production and lauded by our customers.

The third and last block of this is process design and development for manufacturing. This is where the real "nuts and bolts" process work takes place and where Six Sigma tools can really help. We use so-called "Design for Six Sigma" (DFSS) processes to do this. The chaos has gone, the design has been frozen, the Design Verification (DV) builds have been done and now it's on to production. Designing for cost, quality, and process time is the key. We use design failure mode and effects analysis (DFMEA), production failure mode and effects analysis (PFMEA), and Production Verification (PV) builds to help us do this.

How much time do you allocate to innovation?

There's no allocation per se. Most of my life, and I know this is true for lots of people, I'm not in control of everything, and especially not at 3M. Sometimes I think most things are in control of me. [smiles] A few immovable subjects appear on my calendar, such as strategic planning meetings, financial reviews, and the like, that I can do little about. But they are then interspersed by a sort of "make-it-up as you go along" process.

On average, though, I probably spend 5 to 10 percent of my time on innovation. Now what I mean by that is talking to our engineers, talking to our scientists, talking about process, talking about products, talking about scientific breakthroughs, and talking about prioritization. And sometimes I even throw my own (sometimes wacky) ideas at our people. Sorry, but I can't resist the temptation. [smiles] At my time of life, by the grace of the Almighty, I have the privilege of poking my nose in on occasions. And you know what, because the folks who I work with know me well, and know that I'm their principal supporter, they're amazingly tolerant of me. Whether I actually tell them anything useful or not is another matter altogether! That could be debated! [smiles]

What are some possible future innovations at 3M?

In order to get a sense of the future opportunities, I think it's helpful to understand 3M a little. When I first came to 3M, I remember trying to figure out just what 3M was all about, with so many products and so many markets. It's easy to be overwhelmed by it! But the answer is deceptively simple.

About 80 percent of what 3M makes involve what I call backings and coatings. The backings can be woven materials, non-woven materials, plastics, or metal ... any substrate of any kind that you can think of. The coatings can be adhesives, they can be non-woven materials, they can be abrasive particles or they could be optical patterns. We imprint patterns on coatings; we put coatings on backings. We sometimes sell the backings or coatings independently, such as abrasive granules. After coating a product, 3M will imprint special patterns on the surface, sometimes visible and sometimes invisible to the naked eye. These patterns can completely transform the performance of the basic product. We call this process microreplication. That's how most of 3M fundamentally works.

And you see it in something as simple as a Post-it brand note; at its simplest, a piece of paper with some adhesive on the back. Now you might ask, "What's the big deal?" But if you look at this adhesive under a microscope, it looks like a sea of mushrooms. So when you put it down, the tips of the adhesive mushrooms touch the paper. When you lift it up, the elastic forces have to be just a little bit stronger than the tack forces, so it extends and then pulls off the paper cleanly. That way you don't damage the paper or the adhesive and you can reposition the note multiple times. It's so amazing. So even in a simple Post-it note, there's just an amazing amount of technology. And we continue to innovate and find better ways to build that Post-it note.

But the application of this microreplication technology is broad: it's abrasives, it's in micro-needles for replacing syringes, it's in optical films, in fact it's all across our product portfolio.

One extremely promising area beyond microreplication is nanotechnology. We're developing applications for nano materials because the ability of nanotechnologies to completely transform the performance of materials is incredible. Just a week or so after I joined the company, one of the chemists had a jar of calcium carbonate (or something like that) and shook it around in a bottle. And it clumped up and stuck to the inside of the jar. Then he added just a pinch of nano-polymers and the characteristics of the material were completely transformed—it behaved like milk! Whenever you can alter the behavior of materials like that, it opens up all kinds of opportunities in materials science! Some of the folks that work here are either geniuses or magicians. Sometimes I'm not sure which.

What aspects of your business are most likely to change most in the next five years?

That's hard to estimate. That's kind of like betting on the horse races. There's no favorite, and there's no racing form. I think probably healthcare or security would be the answer to the question. But that's purely an educated guess. We won't know that until the day comes.

Will the way 3M approaches innovation change over the next five years?

Well, we have to find ways to become more efficient, to innovate faster and more efficiently. That's a real incongruous kind of statement, based on all I've said before, but the reality is that innovation is happening faster and faster everywhere in the world and, as a company who has made innovation its business, we have to learn to be faster.

The vital need for speed in almost every aspect of business is paramount today. How do you innovate faster, how do you create faster? The answer is you've got to take more risks. So risk management and the acceptance of risk is an incredibly important element of growth and faster innovation. You literally could spend hundred of millions or a billion on something and see it come to nothing. The pharmaceutical business in particular is probably an extreme example of this. Military and defense technologies also come to mind.

So you need to understand that with speed comes risk. One of the classic ways to describe this is, would you rush around at top speed inside a completely dark room when there are poison spikes protruding from every wall? The usual argument of the engineer is, "No way, you can't possibly rush this." My answer is in the modern world of hyper competition at warp speed, you can't possibly not rush it! There has to be some balance between these two extremes of caution and outright abandon. But that's what we do. That's what we all do.

Do you have any advice for other CEOs to improve innovative performance?

It's just an observation that with big rewards come big risks. But in a company like 3M, the only price that's bigger to you than innovating, is not innovating. I remember being asked a question some years ago when I worked at Emerson. Somebody was complaining about the investments we were making in training our people. He asked, "What if we train all these people and they leave?" I said, "What if you don't train them and they stay?" It's the same thing with innovation. You have no choice, however bad it seems. Life in the fast lane of innovation may have its agonies, but it sure beats the alternative.

PATRICK CESCAU
GROUP CEO
UNILEVER

Unilever is one of the leading global manufacturers of fast moving consumer goods. Formed in 1930 following the merger of two existing companies, Unilever today has a portfolio of about 400 brands in 14 foods, home care and personal care categories, including Lipton, Knorr, Dove, and Omo. In 2006, the company invested about €900 million in R&D, representing 2.3 percent of sales revenue, focused on five R&D laboratories and a network of innovation centers all around the world. Recent novel products range from a Lifebuoy hand washing product in India to reduce the amount of rinse water required, to Becel/Flora pro.activ products which are recognized as the most significant advancement in dietary management of cholesterol in four decades. With its Nutrition Enhancement Programme, Unilever has shown its industry leadership by eliminating almost all trans fats from margarine products.

BIOGRAPHY

Mr. Patrick Cescau has been Group Chief Executive of Unilever since April 2005.

He began his career in 1973 when he joined Unilever France as an organization officer. Since then his career has taken him to many countries across the world and he has held senior positions with Unilever in Germany, the Netherlands, Indonesia, Portugal, and the United States.

In May 1999 he was appointed Financial Director of Unilever, a position he held until August 2000 when he moved on to lead the integration of Bestfoods. In January 2001 he took up the position as Director of the company's Global Foods Division. In October 2004, Patrick Cescau was appointed Chairman of Unilever PLC and Deputy Chairman of Unilever N.V., and when Unilever simplified its management structure in April 2005, he was appointed as the first single Group Chief Executive of the Unilever Group.

Patrick Cescau was educated at ESSEC, graduating with a business degree, and later earned an MBA with distinction from INSEAD. Patrick is a Non-Executive Director of Pearson PLC and a Conseiller du Commerce Exterieur de la France in the Netherlands. He was awarded the Legion d'Honneur in January 2005. He is married, has two children, and is a voracious reader, a passable golfer, and a good photographer.

INTERVIEW

[Editors' note: Neal Matheson, Chief Technology Officer, also attended the interview.]
What are the major reasons for Unilever's innovative performance?
First, we will need a bit of humility, because our innovation performance is mixed with some outstanding successes, while we also have, I guess as everybody else, some failures. I think that's important to recognize. The second comment is that one of my roles is to ensure that growth is coming not only from innovation, but also from other sources in the organization. And that's very important to avoid the

company becoming an innovation junkie. Innovation is expensive, it's risky, and there are a lot of other ways to get growth. And that's the ultimate goal—growth which energizes the company. Although a key driver, innovation is not the only way for us to drive growth in our business.

If I look at the reason why perhaps we were successful innovators, it was because we had a clear innovation strategy directly linked to our business strategy. We are very clear about our innovation process, and we are also very disciplined in our process. This requires leadership, especially at the start of new projects. We have a uniform innovation process used throughout the company, which is about ideas, feasibility, capability, and rollout. Projects move from gate to gate, requiring a green light at each check point to move on. We also exert a lot of senior management judgement to assess individual projects at each gate. We don't let a thousand flowers bloom; we prune as necessary. So leadership, discipline, and clarity of strategy. Clarity also as to the technology platform we hope to create and leverage. Post-launch evaluation of new product launches is also important, to learn from your mistakes.

I would add a couple of other points. Innovation is not just something about new products. It is also about a lot of other things linked to our business model. It is about communication, and about rollout, because in the world in which we live, even a great innovation will fail, if you are unable to communicate or are unable to roll out the innovation properly. Of course, in everything we do, we leverage deep, profound consumer insights. Our job is to solve consumer problems, to identify unmet present and future consumer needs and product gaps.

This is all part of what I believe are the key success factors. All that together, I believe is the driving force behind our innovation engine, and behind the success that we are having.

You mentioned it's important to learn from mistakes. Could you elaborate how you measure results?

We measure results in many ways.

First, we link innovation to growth so that our innovation funnel has a value, which is an expectation of turnover, net of cannibalization for some period of time, properly discounted from a risk perspective. That's one important consideration.

We also conduct post-mortems of our launches to understand the reasons for success or failure against our objectives. This is very important because the failure may come from an inability to generate product trial, or it may come from poor repeat rates which may point out a lack of product performance. Trial may simply be a matter of communication, or an issue of distribution which is below the target penetration. Lack of loyalty of the users, under-estimation of competitive reaction, and cost of competing are all considerations.

For each innovation we have a set of key performance indicators that we are following when the innovation is launched. Comparing these with the launch objectives, we determine what is going right and what is going wrong and what should be corrected. So it's a very disciplined system where we track in market performance from a product performance, an attitude performance, and a business performance, and take action.

How would you describe the innovation strategy at Unilever?

The goal is growth. The job can vary depending on a category. In some cases the goal will be to access adjacent categories, by leveraging the brand. To take an example, Dove, which is all about moisturizing cream, started in soap and then expanded into hand and body cream, deodorant and hair care, leveraging a technology platform for moisturization and care.

Launching our deodorants in Russia was a very different challenge. Innovation here was about the way the product impacts the consumer. In this case, we had a lot of controversy for what we did. We pictured a lady with a little piggy in her armpit, to depict odor. That makes the point. So depending upon the objective, there will be a different innovation strategy leveraging relevant consumer insights, brand communication platforms, and technology platforms that we have identified as core to our business.

When we talk about innovation, of course, we talk about a portfolio of innovations. We try to look not only at incremental innovation with incremental benefits, as far as the consumer is concerned, but also at breakthrough innovations, with new technology, offering a new consumer benefit. When we look at a category—we organize our business in categories—like deodorant or hair care, for example, we will try to get a balance, hopefully, within our innovation portfolios. Of course, we would be stupid to have only breakthrough innovation projects or only incremental ones. So, we look for a balanced portfolio in line with the strategy, with different "jobs to be done," depending on what it is we are trying to deliver. So, very flexible. The common things are the process, the alignment, the role of the leadership, and the learning as we go.

Is global reach at Unilever important to stimulating and developing new products?

It is critical, and we have therefore reorganized our business around global categories. The common roles for our category leadership teams cover innovation, branding, brand development, research and development, and innovation, and their job is global. And hence, the way they will work is to identify global consumer opportunities. So if you take Axe [called Lynx in the UK] which I'm sure you're familiar with, the consumer insight is the same in Japan, in the United States, in France, in Germany—how can we help boys in the mating game? That's what it's all about. And this allows us to identify communication platforms, technology platforms that you can deploy with great continuity around the world. Dove is another example; it's all about empowering real beauty—another common global platform.

So we identify global communication platforms and global technology platforms based on global consumer insights. Which doesn't mean that one size fits all, because there are different ways to express these ideas and leverage technology for different markets. If you deal with Asian hair, for example, you will need different approaches than for Caucasian hair. We leverage that—looking for global solutions, but recognizing the differences.

Our infrastructure is global in many ways.

We have global R&D centers, limited in number, and we have innovation centers, spread around the world, aligned with centers of expertise for the category. This being said, I'm more and more convinced that R&D and brand development are going to be more and more linked and interacting together. In other words, if you are dealing with a technology challenge or a consumer challenge in China, the solution is not necessarily about putting more facilities in China. It's all about being able to effectively leverage the totality of your global expertise against this problem.

Do China and India play an important role in your innovation strategy?

Yes, they do, for the following reason. Our turnover in China is about €800 million, growing at about 30 percent, that means €200 million worth of growth per annum. Our turnover in Western Europe is about €12 billion, growing at about 2 percent. You see that both generate about the same amount of growth. In India, our business is over €2 billion. Both India and China represent an extraordinary source of growth and opportunity. We have been in India for 75 years. In China also, but with some interruption, and for this reason our business is smaller. And the challenge in both places – and that is probably something that sets us apart from our competitors – is that we try to address the needs and the aspirations of the consumers across the income pyramid. This means that we sell products to people who earn $2 a day, which requires a very different way of doing business, of leveraging business systems, co-creation and partnership, with a different challenge than we face in a developed market. That's the first comment.

The second comment is that both China and India are extraordinarily complex in terms of consumers. The old stereotype of the Chinese consumer is gone. It has become as complex and segmented as you can imagine, and the environment is very competitive, so you need to put in some of your best resources. It's changing so fast, so dramatically fast in all aspects that you have a moving target, and the pace of innovation is very different. But it still all starts with the consumer. The process is the same, simply there are some big executional differences. Let me give you two examples in India.

We have worked the past eight years on a project called Pure-it which is, in its simplest form, a way to purify water. You can take water from anywhere in India, even from rivers, and put it through our product— it looks like a coffee machine—and you can drink it. It eliminates the bacteria, viruses and even parasites. And that could be an absolute revolution. It has been in tests for the past two to three years, and we're looking at scaling up. And scaling up, as well as a test, means that we have to involve a great number of partners, because there are significant executional challenges. We are not experts in designing the machines. So we look for the right partner here, and the way we manage this innovation project is very different from the way we manage other projects.

The other example I want to mention is a project called Shakti in India, where the innovation was not the product but rather the business model. We have teamed up with a micro-funding group and destitute women to create a business model where we use them as direct sales people. We train them, educate them, and support them, and this way we reach now about 400 million low-income consumers in rural India. So the dimensions of innovation are much broader. We can innovate product form, plus communication, plus distribution, plus go-to-market, plus whatever else. Your scope is going to be very different.

What is your role in advancing innovation?

Because innovation is central to strategy and strategy is basically my domain and that of the top leadership team, it is on my agenda in many ways. First, because I set the standard for the performance of the company, the stretch, the contribution that innovation should make. Second, because my team reviews all the key innovations at an early stage in concept, prototype, or in the form of a finished product—we look at them physically, in terms of product performance, targets, learnings. Third, innovation very much depends on allocation of resources, direction of resources, and leadership, and it requires creating standards for risk management in the company. Because, if you don't accept failure, if you don't encourage risk, it is unlikely that you're going to get great innovation. You need to find ways of being able as a CEO to accept failure, to visibly recognize that that's part of the game, not all the time, not the same failure all the time. But trying to create this environment I believe is important. You have to be the champion of innovation, and be visibly engaged in the innovation process.

Could you give me a recent example and the role you played?

Pure-it is a very good example. I've been following this project for the past two years and in my last visit to India I decided that we will not go for competitive advantage, but for reputational advantage because in the time that you and I have spoken, I don't know how many children die from lack of access to water. You need to make a choice as to whether you're going to scale up rapidly and save the world, or whether you're going to keep it close and use the technology for our competitive advantage. That brings me to a point which is perhaps even more important. I said the CEO has to champion things and send signals. That's a signal. Open innovation and co-creation would be two other signals that we would send loud and clear.

There is one other area which, more and more, I have championed personally in speeches, for example at INSEAD and at Columbia Business School, which is that I am absolutely convinced that the future of business is one where you do well and you do good at the same time. And hence, we have dramatically increased the sustainability and other social innovation content of what we produce. Let me explain what I mean by that. With brands you need to satisfy not only the functional needs of your consumer, you need to meet their emotional needs, and more and more you need also to meet their needs as citizens. So we innovate in laundry detergent by producing detergent powder which uses 50 percent less water and reduced rinsing in the wash process, or dramatically less packaging. Or we innovate in tea by selling sustainable tea coming from certified plantations, ones where children are not involved in labor and where the level of protection is similar to what we give to our own employees on our own plantations. And that more and more I believe is going to be a hallmark of future innovation and future brand positioning.

How do you compensate innovation?

It's both individual and team, this is our approach. We don't have a different process for innovation. The only thing that we do in parallel is that we have a venture group, where we have partners who are venture capitalists. We look at technologies at the boundaries of our business, and then of course the rewards are very different, and our involvement is also very different. That's part of the driver of innovation, to use venture funds to access technology which wouldn't be on our radar screen, or that we would be unable to nurture within our organization.

How is an individual compensated for an idea?

If your job is a marketing or brand development job, your job is to innovate. If you're doing a fabulous job, you will be rewarded through the success of the brands. But you're not going to be rewarded very specifically for the idea. It may be that there is an emotional reward, you get a prize and are celebrated. But as we believe that a lot of the innovations are a collective act, we reward teams.

If you look back over the past five years, have there been changes as to how you approach innovation?

By and large, not in terms of process, because to a certain extent the process is just discipline. A number of things are on my agenda. First, to increase research efficiency and increase the output of research. Second, to drive open innovation. Third, as I indicated, much more emphasis on sustainability and social innovation. Fourth, because of the huge change in raw material prices, much more time and resources devoted to delivering the same benefit at lower cost. And fifth, a much more structured approach to innovation strategy and innovation platforms, technology platforms. And all that, to sum up, is why I decided to bring Neal Matheson to Unilever as our Chief Technology Officer, so he could embody this change, which is in fact rebalancing the very strong focus and strong integration between brands and technology strategy, but also to leverage more innovation platforms and identify the next generations of technology for all categories.

What changes do you foresee over the next five years?

Sustainability, as I say, is going to be more and more on the agenda. If there is no water, there is no detergent powder. If there's no fish, there are no fish fingers. The second is the opportunities at the bottom of the pyramid, addressing the needs of lower-income consumers, because of our developing and emerging market orientation. The third is our belief in the functional benefits of consumer products. If I look at the number of big technological changes, there's not been too many in our industry. I believe that this is going to change. Physics, for example, will revolutionize personal care. I believe that diagnostic medicine, diagnostic kits, and all the rest of it will impact our business. Genomics is already impacting our business and research, and in a similar way nanotechnologies and micro factories will be part of our business. This is why I thought it was very important to get ahead of the curve and put a renewed emphasis on long-term commitments and bets in technology in a different way through open innovation, co-creation, and the other ways we were talking about earlier.

You mentioned that sustainability is a challenge for the future. How do you as CEO and a company respond?

First, I mentioned our leadership community knows it is important, and I do that internally and externally by taking advantage of communication opportunities. So I went to INSEAD, and to Colombia Business School, [indicating his desk filled with prizes] and got this beautiful prize. In today's world, if I do a speech at Columbia Business School, the next day I receive emails from our people in Kenya or in Saudi to talk to me. I receive letters from people I've never heard of, so that's one. Second is again setting expectations, and being very clear as to the return of the innovation process and the position of our brand. So how do we do that? We have developed a new methodology called brand imprint, where we look at the world from the perspective of our brand in a 360-degrees way—social, economic, environmental. We piloted this with four or five of our brands, and now we are extending it to all brands. As a team, our top leadership team, we're going to do the same exercise for the Unilever brand. Last, but not least, we've put Vitality at the heart of our mission. So it's the mission of the company, we communicate, set expectations and direction, and we role model, and of course influence the development of processes. So the mindset, processes, deliverables, are clearly identified and actioned.

Do you think it's important to partner with more external actors?

It's essential; it's not important, it's essential. And one of the reasons that Neal Matheson is here as Chief Technology Officer is because I want to accelerate that. It's essential because there's a lot of science out there that we need to capture and align. We need to get better at it. We can't do what we were doing 20 years ago, which was to control all the technology and sub-technology necessary for us to do the job. We also need to look externally because, just like outsourcing, some others may do parts of the job better than we do, because of their skills, their competence, and their vision. You just need to be in control of the network.

Academia is changing too. We see an American professor, he gives you two business cards. One for professor of science at University of Santa Barbara, say, and the second for a start-up company that may compete with you. So there is much more coming from technology. The big problem is that all these Ph.D.s can't understand why the business people have stolen leadership for all these years. Now they're coming back with a vengeance, they're coming, being very creative, very business-like. We need to tap into that. So, network.

The job of the science today for me is as much about defining the network and being in control of the network. There's going to be stuff in it which we will do ourselves, because that's where we will derive our competitive advantage. For the rest, we take it from the best. And we do that in advertising, we do that in communication, we do that in the way we run our business, and we should do that exactly the same in science.

What about partnering with key competitors?
We partner with PepsiCo for Lipton ready-to-drink tea because our strengths here are complementary. They have the go-to-market capability in bottling and distribution, and we have the brand and the technology. So there's a mutual benefit. If you partner with a competitor, either it is an area which is irrelevant from one point of view and I don't know why they or we should be involved, or it is an area which is interesting and relevant for both, and assuming there is no anti-trust challenge, it can be a sustainable way, because you can't be friends on one little area and try

83

to rip at each other's heart in the rest of the business. Trust won't be there.

Do you think it might change in the future?

What's going to change, in my view, is that just like with globalization and the Internet, you're going to partner with people that in the past you would have had no idea you were going to partner with. So when we develop our pyramid tea bags, we partner with a cigarette company, because, we say, wait a second, if this guy can produce these cigarettes with this performance in terms of output per minute, why can't we use the technology to produce our little tea bag, and we work together to use the same technology. That works. I see us partnering with people we are not competing with, but who can provide us with capabilities that we don't have and for which there is mutual benefit. I see us partnering with competitors on sustainability issues—in water, for example, I could see us partnering with Nestlé, that's possible. I see us partnering more and more with complementors, they provide finance, raw materials etc. Co-creating on innovation, I see that happening, more so as innovation and the Internet offer fabulous opportunities to bring the technology that you need. More and more we see opportunities. So how to do Wikipedia in product design for Unilever?

When we acquired Ben & Jerry's, I remember asking the first time I went there, "What's your process for generating ideas?" And there were some 5,000 ideas for new products per quarter from their consumers. They love the company and they say, hey, have you thought about a new ice cream called, what have you, Che Guevara, all the components coming from Cuba? So, in my view that will be the future, the future we need to rethink. It won't be about bricks and mortar, it will be about networking, flexibility, co-creation, open innovation, that's my vision. As I'm not able to realize it alone, I take competent external people to bring that about.

You talked about food, cosmetics. In which areas do you foresee the most changes in the next five years?

Probably in the areas of food and personal care. Food because vitality and well-being—good for you, better for you—is where we are all going. And personal care because I believe technology will impact dramatically. So the first one, if you want to reformulate a product with a lot of salt without losing the taste, that's a tough technological challenge. The product has to be good, otherwise the people simply add salt, which is not the objective. Nanotechnology has an opportunity to deposit conditioning, fragrances, or whatever, where you want it, when you want it. There will be a lot of physics impacting personal care. There will be much more technology in personal care in years to come.

Do you need to do something different in a recession?

The answer should be, no, you should not do anything different. The reality though is, if I look at what we are doing, part of the budget has moved to delivering the same benefit at much lower cost. That's tough, and that's useful, but clearly the proportion of such projects have increased because if you have the mineral oil price at $100, that's tough. We are reducing the fat content in mayonnaise or margarine because edible oil prices are going through the roof. So the answer is you're not cutting budget, that we're never doing. But within that, there may be a reallocation of resources, tougher choices, and also recognizing that the environment has changed, that you need to understand what it means for your business and have the flexibility to react.

How does the innovation platform lead to innovation and manufacturing?

[Matheson] You'll just create networks at both stages. If you think in term of a scientist being accountable for these superior technologies, say in a benefit space. They can't do it themselves. So by definition they have to know what's going on around them, and they have to create the networks that they're going to need to deliver the superior approach. Once they generate a lead and we start identifying target brands and countries, then we have to deliver it; that requires a different network, probably different people. It will pass on down the cycle. But if you just take a typical funnel, as it goes down the funnel, what used to be is everybody tried to do as much as they can in-house.

What we want to do now, obviously, and what we are doing is finding partners. But I think Patrick's view of the network is a lot more powerful, because then you're not just then creating one partner, you're thinking in terms of where's the win and where can I get the very best at whatever point that I need it? So it's about speed, it's about superiority, it's about cost, and so we need people who are much, much broader than we would typically have had in a standard R&D organization where you had people who are narrowly focused on the science, on the execution, on a claims support. Here you're saying, no, you own this space, all the technical space, you have to understand it and be accountable for delivery. So in a sense you have to start training R&D people from the start as business leaders.

[Cescau] That's a very important point. If I go and review a series of innovation projects coming out of our labs, in the past, I guess the group in charge of the innovation would have shown me all the technology, sub-technology. All would be their stuff. We had people 15, 20 years ago that were close to a Nobel prize. That will never happen again. Because today, we say, show me the progress. I have in front of me a big network with suppliers for materials involved, designers, fragrance experts, and there will be 35 or 40 different entities working to the command of the lead researcher, or the project leader, to deliver the goods. Hence we need specialists, just like an orchestra, but we need more and more conductors putting that all together on time, in full.

Let me give an example from deodorants. We spent a lot of money trying to develop new technology to improve aerosols. I remember the first time I saw this stuff, I realized how much money I would spend, I said I don't think this is going to work. It's taking too much time and we're not making enough progress. And, lo and behold, one year later, a third-party group under our management delivered a perfect solution at a fraction of the cost. And that focuses the mind of the people.

This is why the issue of research efficiency is extraordinarily important, because that's where you're going to start understanding that you have a problem. The platform is extremely important, if you commit, and we look at—that's another change—a longer time horizon. You need to have reassurance of the structure of delivery and technology on the way to support your launches and re-launches. And that requires that you have mapped pretty well your research plan, and you can feel confident you can deliver to this calendar. Otherwise we would have promised things to our customers and our consumer and not be able to deliver. That's a big change.

[Matheson] Many people think of open innovation as somehow manna dropping from heaven, you're going to get these wonderful innovations from other people but it doesn't happen this way. We create the network, we own that space, we find the experts and that's how you tap the full value of the opportunity.

What are the limits to innovation?

The capability to execute. There are several things. First, the customer. We see a number of so-called innovations, and the number that failed with the consumer is mind-boggling, it's a lot. Over the past couple of years we've dramatically reduced—like from five to one—the number of projects in our innovation funnels, because more and more, we need fewer projects that will make a bigger impact, to avoid all the clutter. And help with the capability to execute. Do you realize that, theoretically, in the first quarter of 2008, we should be talking about our 2010 innovation plans with our customers, staff, and in some cases co-creating with them?

[Matheson] Don't think in terms of executional capability as traditional, because what we're trying to do is make our own competitive approach. And I totally agree with Patrick, that's exactly where the bottleneck is. But it's because there's innovation required in executing too. You can't just execute the way everybody else is, you'll never be heard above all the clutter. So it takes tremendous skill, and we have to learn how to start earlier.

[Cescau] That's one of the big lessons. We need to extend our planning horizon, which has all sorts of implications in terms of risk, in terms of number of bets, size of the bet, in terms of alignment. It's one thing to align three months before launch, it's another thing one year before launch, and an even bigger thing two and a half years before launch. If we could say now, do you agree that in 2010 this will be our portfolio of innovations that we're going to put on the market, everybody would love that, especially our customers. And, by the way, some of the technology is not yet fully developed, some of the communication is not visible, we might have some prototype, and some consumer research, but still a long way to go. It will require a very different stance for the management. It's interesting and difficult at the same time. Things are moving faster all the time, and to say we have to plan more in advance, longer planning cycles, makes it more difficult. That's one of the challenges we have got.

[Matheson] This is why you need platforms as Patrick was saying earlier, because platforms allow you to focus for a longer time horizon, you're focusing on a continuous growth in a specific benefit area. So you can have more clarity, you can help manage that whole process over time. *What advice can you give other CEOs to improve innovation performance?*

[Cescau] The first thing I would say is that he or she needs to show to the organization that innovation is important, that he's really the champion. Because if the CEO is not role modeling, if people don't take their cues from their leader, and if the CEO doesn't seem passionate about the brand, about innovation, about growth, then it is not going to be important for the organization. The second thing I would say, probably the most important job is to set a direction, to clarify the strategy, to define expectations. The third thing is to be clear that innovation doesn't happen by accident. There is rigor and discipline in the innovation process. He needs to be clear that it is a top leadership activity, one that needs to be managed from the top, because if you don't, somebody else or many others will manage it through the organization, and then you're not all pulling in the same direction. Other people at much different levels and for many different reasons will decide what your innovation policies are, and that's not good. The last advice I would give is that the CEO needs to create an environment which is conducive of innovation; it's not only about discipline and process, it is also about risk, it is also about challenge, about limiting and avoiding bureaucracy and everything which stifles creativity.

FUJIO CHO

CHAIRMAN

TOYOTA MOTOR CORPORATION

Toyota is the world's largest producer of cars and the most profitable automobile manufacturer. Headquartered in Aichi, Japan, and founded as a separate company from the Toyota group in 1937, the company today has more than 500 subsidiaries. In addition to passenger cars, minivans, and trucks, the company produces a wide range of IT-based systems, such as car multimedia systems, on-board intelligent systems, advanced transportation systems, and transportation infrastructure and logistics systems. Toyota markets its vehicles under the Toyota and Lexus brands, as well as through the Scion line of automobiles sold in the United States. In FY2007, Toyota invested 890 billion yen in R&D, representing 3.7 percent of consolidated net revenue. The company has 11 major R&D sites worldwide. Innovation has been a hallmark of its just-in-time manufacturing process, and more recent innovations include an Advanced Parking Guidance System for automatic parking, a four-speed, electronically controlled automatic transmission offering power and economy, an eight-speed automatic transmission, and Prius, the world's first mass-produced and best-selling hybrid gas-electric vehicle.

BIOGRAPHY

Fujio Cho has been instrumental in honing Toyota's production system throughout his career. He later put that knowledge to work in distribution control and on the project team that coordinated the preparations for Toyota's plant in Kentucky, its first plant in North America. Mr. Cho also has extensive experience in government and industrial affairs, having worked in a supporting role, until 1998, at the Japan Federation of Economic Organizations (Keidanren), which was at the time headed by then Toyota Motor Corporation (TMC) Chairman Shoichiro Toyoda.

A graduate of the Faculty of Law at the University of Tokyo, Mr. Cho joined Toyota upon earning his degree in 1960. After spending his early career in General Affairs, in 1974 he became a manager in the Production Control Division, where he was assigned to the Operations Management Consulting Department to learn the principles of the Toyota Production System (TPS) from TPS authority Taichi Ohno. In 1984, Mr. Cho became a department general manager in the Logistic Management Division, while co-serving as a project general manager in the Production Control Division.

In 1987, Mr. Cho was dispatched to Kentucky, USA as executive vice president at Toyota Motor Manufacturing, Kentucky, Inc. (TMMK). He was named a Toyota director in 1988, and later that year, he became president of TMMK. He returned to Japan in 1994, where he was named a managing director, and he became a senior managing director in 1996. In 1998, Mr. Cho became an executive vice president, where he oversaw Toyota's corporate planning, information systems, and industrial equipment. Mr. Cho was president of TMC from 1999 to 2005. As the company's head, he not only shaped corporate policy for Toyota, but also served as a spokesman for the automobile industry and for manufacturing in general. In June

2005, he assumed the position of a vice chairman at TMC, before becoming chairman in June 2006.

In 2005, Mr. Cho was appointed a vice chairman of the Japan Business Federation (Nippon Keidanren) and he assumed chairmanship of the Japan Automobile Manufacturers Association (JAMA) in 2006.

In 2004, the French government honored him with the Ordre national de la Legion d'Honneur, *and in 2006, he was also honored with Knight Commander, the Most Excellent Order of the British Empire.*

Mr. Cho enjoys golf and fishing, and likes listening to classical music. Mr. Cho was born in 1937. He grew up in Tokyo, but presently resides in Toyota City, Aichi Prefecture, with his wife, Emiko. The Chos have two sons.

INTERVIEW

[Editors' note: The interview was conducted through a translator.]
What are the major reasons for Toyota's innovative performance?
I believe when we're talking about innovation, we have to first of all make clear how we recognize and define innovation. And so to start with, when we talk about innovation in my company, one type of innovation that is extremely critical is the innovation that is related to technological development. To put it another way, this is the innovation that you can find in our products. And when we work on the areas like production engineering or production planning, innovation is a very important part of the process. So in the process of manufacturing innovation is very critical.

To start with, let's talk about innovation related to the products of Toyota and our R&D activities. The main reason (for innovation), I have to mention, is the change in the business environment that was triggered by global warming. I believe the automotive industry needs to play a major role in offering solutions to the worldwide problems related to this issue.

This (change in business environment) is specifically manifested in the laws and regulations of the countries in the world where we sell automobiles. Europe announced introduction of a 140 gram per kilometer CO_2 emission restriction by the year 2008 and 2009. Similar restrictions are either being introduced or are becoming more severe in countries like the United States, China, and Japan as well. If automotive manufacturers fail to properly address such external restrictions, I am afraid they will cease to exist.

Another change (in business environment) is the situation, which happened to Toyota, where hybrid vehicles became very popular among customers, and sales exploded in an instant. In this case, the Toyota brand got improved recognition as a brand that excels in environment technology and is zealously applying this technology in its work. Improvement of brand image increased not only the sales of hybrid vehicles, but other models as well.

So, coming back to your original question, I believe the simple answer to what are the reasons for my company's innovative performance is: "competing against difficult situations that need attention."

I believe there are various scenarios or possible sets of circumstances in which innovation would take place. When I think of the current environment that surrounds the automotive industry, first of all there are various types of needs. We are totally absorbed by working on answers to those needs. There is no other choice, but make the needs our first priority.

There is another starting point for innovation: that is creating new ideas from the seed level.

But, for the moment, our strength is in starting our R&D activities from the needs and developing answers to those needs. I'd go even further; I believe I am not mistaken saying that innovation based on needs is faster, cheaper, and a more dependable approach.

What is your role to help advance innovation?

This is a bit related to my background. From my very young days I have been involved in production engineering and manufacturing. Our (Toyota Motor Corporation) approach to manufacturing is called "lean manufacturing" or "Toyota Production System." In the field of manufacturing as well as in production engineering Toyota's style is a big innovation in itself. It took us 40–50 years to establish.

In this area (Toyota Production System) my role was human resource development. I was particularly responsible for ensuring that this system in Toyota matched the mandate and the requirement of the times. To make it happen, I needed to decide "who" within the company should be assigned to "what" kind of position, and to "whom" should we teach what.

At the same time I was assigned to evaluate all 52 overseas production plants to identify which ones were lagging behind or which specific site needed to catch up. Applying pressure to those facilities was my additional role.

On the other hand, when it comes to technological R&D, I am not really familiar with specific details. Therefore, my role was to clarify, first of all, the set of needs that currently exist, so that we can identify what kind of product we have to supply. In this regard, I believe my role was to extract out of the R&D department the technologies that can be materialized into a prototype and put them into a test-drive for evaluation.

That was exactly what my predecessor, Mr. Okuda did

with Prius—Toyota's hybrid vehicle—in 1997, when he was the CEO. So Mr. Okuda as the CEO had extracted these technologies out of R&D and actually materialized this into Prius.

During my time as CEO, when the fuel cell technology was ripe for actual prototyping, I ordered production of 20 vehicles. Ten of them were sent to the United States, the remaining ten units were test driven in Japan. During a year of test-driving we managed to identify practical issues that needed improvement.

Repeating sentences like: "This is exactly what we need" and "Hurry up! We need it as fast as possible!" is what I continue to see as my role.

How do you compensate innovative individuals?

Maybe it's somewhat difficult for those of you living in the Western world to understand the culture in Japanese corporations, because I think Japanese companies are somewhat different from US or European counterparts.

In a Japanese company it is very rare to compensate an individual. We do have an internal "Employee Improvement Suggestion System," that rewards employees each time they come with a good improvement proposal related to their everyday work. But this is related to rather small *Kaizen* or continuous improvement.

However, when it comes to a major development, like our hybrid vehicle Prius, not an individual, but a development project team developed it. In such a case, it is not our practice to actually reward individual team members.

What are the main innovative challenges facing Toyota?

I'm not really sure whether my answer would suffice, but to start with, I believe not only Toyota, but the whole automotive industry is placed in a very tough and difficult environment. One example: automotive manufacturers have to come up with new innovative products, one after another, that fully take into account the need to address the global environmental issues. And this, of course, requires an enormous amount of innovation.

The difficult side of this innovation is the existence of multiple approaches to address, in an automobile, the global environmental issue. To be more specific, in addressing the environmental issues, there are various alternative technologies that we can adopt. So we currently have, as an alternative, an electric vehicle, fuel cell vehicle, hydrogen-fueled vehicle, bio-fuel, and also we have the hybrid vehicle, which is a combination of gasoline engine and electric batteries. There are other possibilities as well. At the moment, nobody knows which technology will be used in future as the standard. To master all these technologies up to the point of providing a popular product means that we need vast amounts of capital and people. For the technological R&D activities it would be really a daring judgment, or, should I say, a major adventure for a company like us to determine what specific technology to go ahead with, and just concentrate the managerial resources on that specific technology.

Another challenge related to managerial environment is the rapid progress of globalization. New markets are created, competition intensifies, and if that was not enough, new competitors from China and Korea are entering the market. As the result, we get a dramatic change both in competition and in the business environment in which the automotive industry is working.

To keep up with the change, we have to continue answering the special needs that competition is imposing. It is absolutely vital that we keep innovating and that our R&D divisions relentlessly bring forward new solutions. Without a slightest delay we have to invest human and financial resources to keep up with the speed of global markets. Yet, it seems that time is against us, forcing us to hurry even more.

I cited only two examples to answer your question about challenges for Toyota's innovation, but I believe there are a few more.

Under such intense conditions, it is impossible to settle down, relax, and concentrate without haste on finding a solution. We are forced to think while we're running. This situation in itself is a challenge that we have to face.

What advice can you recommend to CEOs to improve innovative performance?

I think the basic principle is nothing new, so what is important for the CEOs regarding innovation is that there has to be a clear direction set for the people in the company. To be more specific, a CEO needs to clearly state by when and what kind of a solution needs to be created. The remaining task for a CEO is to follow up on this. There's nothing new in that.

What I can suggest in addition are several principles that have to be followed by the employees.

The first one is *Genchi Genbutsu*. (This means going and seeing for yourself to thoroughly understand a situation.) The person who is responsible for creating a prototype has to actually try to use or move it with their very own hands. She or he needs to personally check and personally apply or at least personally supervise application of necessary corrections.

The next principle is to perform sufficient number of tests, launch the product into the market, and commercialize it as fast as possible. Striking a good balance between testing and introducing the product into market is very important. You should not cut corners and try to reduce the number of tests—you might fail to identify critical problems.

But, on the other hand, if you just keep on with your

testing, take too much time, and if there is a delay in commercialization and the launch of the product, that's also not good. Because, the idea would only remain as a desktop theory, while you lose a business chance. It is difficult to strike a proper balance between both activities.

Another important function of the CEO is to regularly visit the R&D sites and talk to people working in the R&D area, checking how they are doing.

What role do China or India play in innovation?
When I think about what role people of China or India play in the process of innovation, their role, at present, is not predominant in regard to Toyota's product or manufacturing process. However, I place great expectation on these countries for the future. That is because I hear that the young generation in countries like China and India is very enthusiastically and diligently studying. I hear opinions that they are very skilled at using technology and IT knowledge. That makes me place a great expectation on the people in these countries.

Now that I have mentioned China and India, although I know that this is not necessarily a response to the gist of your question, I would like to especially add that to develop and produce automobiles that can be sold in markets like India requires an enormous amount of innovative technology. That is because in markets like India we need to develop compact, very inexpensive vehicles with reasonable quality levels. This is something that, I have to admit, Toyota is not really experienced with. This is a new area of technology, or rather a new area of development that we are pursuing at the moment. It cannot be achieved using a traditional approach. Selling cars in India requires use of numerous new technologies. This itself calls for an incredible innovation.

Do you also cooperate and network with universities and research institutes, as well as competitors?

Yes we do. Our technical and R&D divisions collaborate with many universities and research institutions both at home and abroad. Our R&D people either work together with researchers on a specific research theme, or ask these external researchers to come up with a specific technological achievement. Talking about competitors, there is a so-called CAT (Cars equipped with Advanced Technology) project that we are undertaking together with General Motors. This is an environmental project in which we exchange information.

Would a recession introduce changes in innovation policies?

The basic answer is that we won't change anything at a time of recession. However, it would be a different story if a company totally runs out of money. Therefore, utilizing good days, a company should secure reserves, preparing for some tight liquidity in the future.

You see, we cannot stop investing. Toyota spends about 800 billion to 900 billion yen per annum for R&D. Over half of it is used to invent solutions to environmental issues. In this age of fierce competition, we cannot allow ourselves to reduce investment.

What changes do you foresee over the next five years for Toyota and the automotive industry?

In five years, I don't foresee a significant change.

Considering all the different subjects that we are working on at present, will there be an extraordinary improvement, or will there be a dramatic breakthrough? Personally speaking, I don't think so.

But there is one possibility I need to mention. If a battery, not an ordinary battery, but a totally revolutionary, superb, high-performance battery is developed, then in the instant, everything will change.

If an efficient battery is developed, will Toyota have to change?
"Change" meaning that we will start doing things in a different way? No. On the contrary. You see, we are spending billions of yen on R&D, but still cannot focus on only one—the most efficient technology. If a new-generation battery appears, then we are free to focus, to concentrate only on items related to those batteries. This will result in great R&D efficiency. We will be able to achieve significant results in our research. Automatically, company management will also become efficient. We will no longer have to bleed off our finances and personnel into so many different channels.

Unfortunately, there is one difficult problem in this matter. If a breakthrough battery is invented, then auto manufacturers worldwide will face a dilemma: what to do with all the engine factories that use all those materials, machining, assembling, when they might no longer be required with the advent of the batteries?

[Editors' note: Additional materials submitted in writing.]

How is your company using its global reach to stimulate and develop innovative products and services?
Due to our business expansion, many people with various values started to work for Toyota. Toyota values and ways of doing things, which until then had been transferred in a manner that relied on unspoken understanding, could not be tacitly transferred any more. Therefore, we decided to stipulate the values and skills particular for Toyota into a written "Toyota Way" that we could share with all Toyota employees around the world.

What significant issues have you faced in developing new business models?
I am not sure if we can call it a business model, but when global growth accelerated at Toyota, values and skills that were until that point transferred as an unspoken code of

conduct, rapidly absorbed by new hires, became difficult to tacitly transfer. Therefore, we summarized the core values and skills into a manual and distributed it throughout all our offices. We called this manual "Toyota Way."

How do you assess innovation strategies and practices, and measure results?

Realization of innovation at Toyota is a part of the common values expressed in the "Toyota Way." Based on these values, each division is autonomously implementing activities related to innovation. There is no need for a top executive to micromanage each single approach. The results of such voluntary innovation management show, for example, in product quality, in customer satisfaction, and production efficiency, which is continuously monitored within the company. As an effect, there is no additional need to implement new ways of measuring results.

Within Toyota, who are the key decision makers allocating resources to innovative investments? On what basis do they make their investment decisions?

Whenever it is necessary, "everyday *Kaizen*" is individually implemented based on decisions within each division. When there is a need for a big investment, then based on the proposal from the division in charge, all other related divisions with top executives get together in order to discuss and decide details.

FRANZ FEHRENBACH

CEO

BOSCH

The Bosch Group is a leading global supplier of products and services in automotive and industrial technologies, consumer goods, and building technology. Founded in 1886 in Stuttgart, Germany, the Bosch Group today comprises more than 300 subsidiary and regional companies in some 50 countries. In 2007 the company spent more than €3.6 billion on R&D, representing nearly 8 percent of sales revenue. Bosch has nine global corporate research locations, five of which are based in Germany. Among the host of innovations brought forth by the company over time are its first major success, the high-voltage magneto ignition system with spark plug (1902), and the first diesel injection pump for passenger cars (1927). More recently, they include the ABS antilock braking system (1978), high-pressure diesel injection (1989), and the ESP® electronic stability program (1995).

BIOGRAPHY

*Franz Fehrenbach joined Bosch in 1975 after graduating from the University of Karlsruhe that same year with a degree in engineering management (*Wirtschaftsingenieur*). For the next five years he held a series of positions in manufacturing plants before* *joining the Corporate Department for Planning and Controlling as Vice President in 1982. Three years later he moved to the United States to serve as Vice President and subsequently Executive Vice President, Finance and Administration at the Robert Bosch Automotive Group (USA).*

In 1989 he returned to Germany as Vice President, Finance and Administration of the Starters and Alternators division, and was appointed Division President in 1994. Two years later he became Executive Vice President of the Diesel Systems Division, and the following year assumed responsibilities as President, Diesel Systems Division. He was appointed to the Board of Management as deputy member in 1999, becoming a full member in 2001. In 2003, Fehrenbach was appointed Chairman of the Board and CEO.

He is a member of the managing board of the VDA (German Association of the Automotive Industry), of the US Board of the Presiding Committee of the BDI (Federation of German Industries), of the Asia Pacific Committee of German Business and of the BBUG (Baden-Baden Entrepreneurs' Conference). He is also a member of the Senate of the Max Planck Society and of the supervisory board of BASF SE. In 2006 he won the "Eco-manager of the Year Award," presented by WWF Germany and Capital *magazine.*

Franz Fehrenbach was born in Kenzingen (Breisgau), Germany. He is married, and has three sons.

INTERVIEW

What are the major reasons for Bosch's innovative performance?
I can see five major reasons why our company is so innovative. First, and most importantly, we have the mindset that is a must in any company that wants to be innovative. An

innovation culture has to start at the top. But only if it is communicated consistently and over a long period of time, and only if it regularly produces good results in practice, will this idea penetrate the whole company—level by level. Communication starts with a company's vision, mission, and values, but it is crucial that senior management manifest these values in everyday business practice. Then, in the end, all associates will see that management mean what they say. If you remain faithful to these principles in business practice, everybody will be convinced that they work in a company that is innovative and can become a technology leader.

At Bosch, we have published our vision and values in our "House of Orientation" brochure. There, Bosch is presented as a leading technology and services company. But "leading" means more to us than just being a market leader. We want to influence the path technology takes in the business fields we are involved in. We want to shape the future. That's our understanding of "leading." As our vision says, our ambition is to enhance the quality of life with solutions that are both innovative and beneficial for society— solutions that are "Invented for life," as we say in our slogan. In our vision, therefore, there are clear links to innovation and to technology.

Our mission is summed up in a single concept: BeQIK. "Be" stands for operating result (from the German *Betrieb-sergebnis,* "Q" for quality, "I" for innovation, and "K" for customer orientation (from the German *Kundenorien-tierung*). This means we seek continuous improvement, and see this as a way of being better than our competitors. "BeQIK, Be Better, Be Bosch" is an important element of the House of Orientation.

These are just words in a brochure, you might say. Well, let's look at the facts. Over the last 10, 15 years, our expenditure in R&D has remained on a consistently high level, varying by only 1.3 percent in relation to sales, which themselves have more than tripled over this time period. In 2007, total R&D investment was in the region of 8 percent of Bosch Group sales. In the automotive business, this figure was even higher, at more than 10 percent. You will not find a lot of companies in this business that can match these figures. Our researchers and development engineers know that cutting the R&D budget is the last thing we'll do. However, this policy does not prevent us from working continuously on improving our development processes and on adding to our know-how so that we arrive at a better understanding of the context in which we carry out our research and development work. My colleagues and I are convinced that it is vitally important to invest in innovations, irrespective of how the earnings of Bosch develop. This is what I meant when I spoke about mindset: first expressed in the vision, mission, and values, then communicated consistently, and finally borne out by facts. And the facts are that with a total of 3,281 patent applications in 2007, we are the technological leader in Germany. In automotive technology, we are number one in Europe—not only at the European Patent Office, but also at the World Intellectual Property Organization (WIPO).

The second reason is conviction. We share a strong conviction in this company that innovation really is the basis of our future success. And again this starts with senior management. Senior management is the source of the support and the financial resources that are needed to develop the company's different areas of activity. Seeking new solutions day by day demands a lot of consistency, and consistency demands strong convictions. Admittedly, cultivating such convictions in a large, international, and highly diversified company is sometimes far from easy.

Third, we have the right working environment and business organization. To be innovative, you need first-rate, creative, hard-working associates, best-in-class equipment, the right connections, and locations around the world to build up a global network.

The fourth reason is adequate finance. There is nothing worse than when innovation teams are just on the roll and have to stop because there are not enough funds. This really destroys the creative flow. Looking around in the world you can see why companies underperform. They start a lot of new projects and promising innovations, but as soon as a financial crisis threatens they stop everything and return to the products and services they already know. Later on, these companies are no longer competitive. Financial backing must be consistent and reliable. That's why operating result is so important for us, the "Be" in our mission statement.

And finally, we are efficient. An organization that works well today will not necessarily work well tomorrow. Adjustments therefore have to be made continuously. Some of these adjustments are only minor—small steps of the kind that are typical in any continuous improvement process. But sometimes larger steps are needed. There must always be a balance between highly efficient processes and adequate resources.

How do you ensure that a proper mindset is propagated throughout the organization?

Bosch has always been a value-driven company. At the end of the 1990s, however, we realized there was a need for the "Bosch way" to be defined explicitly. We started with a mission statement, because we thought this was something the organization could adopt easily. BeQIK, Be Better, Be

Bosch: quality, innovation, customer orientation. At that time, there were some skeptics who said that if we wrote this down we could be held to account for it. But this was exactly what we wanted. Then there were those who said that missions were for nice times, for good times. I disagree. For me, exactly the opposite is true. It is precisely in critical times that mission statements prove their worth. Later, we followed this up by defining our value code and our vision, and by combining these with our core competencies and business processes to form the House of Orientation.

How do you apply global reach to advance innovation?

Our research and development is still centered in Germany. About two-thirds of our roughly 30,000 engineers are located here. But there were two clear reasons we had to locate research and development outside Germany as well. First of all, in the basic research we had to go to Palo Alto, to Japan, to Singapore, and to all the other technology clusters that are important for us. In the beginning this was mainly scouting. Later on we increased capacity and started up engineering activities in these regions, with their excellent connections to institutions, to universities and so on.

Second, Bosch has always followed its customers, ever since the company was created. We have been present in the United States for more than 100 years, for example, in China since 1909, in Japan since 1911, and so on and so forth. We started with application work, where it made sense to be close to the customer. Research and development followed later.

Could you give me an example of moving into markets outside Europe?

Three years ago we decided to go into the low-price vehicle segment. Why? One obvious reason is the tough cost targets in this segment. They require solutions that will never be found in the premium class. But if these solutions one day become so smart that they can also be applied to the middle-class segment, they could be very dangerous for us. So we will supply parts for the Nano, a car that Tata Motors sells for a base price of €1,700. We deliver the fuel injection system, the brakes, and the starter.

Parts for cars like the Nano must be developed near their future markets, in close cooperation with our local customer, and not in Germany. So the diesel injection system for the Nano is developed in Bangalore, in India, by local teams that remain in close contact with their counterparts in Germany. By relocating our development work in this way, we can avoid some of the mistakes we made in the past. What we have learned in the meantime, however, is that such local development teams come up with solutions we would never have found in Europe. This demonstrates that "low-price R&D" is not just about stripping functions, but can be true innovation. We took a similar approach with FlexFuel in Brazil, the first country to offer the choice of ethanol or gasoline. I'm sure there are lessons to be learned here for other development projects. And it is important that we learn these lessons, and not an upcoming local competitor. This will be another positive side-effect.

Do you need a different mindset for low-price R&D?

The low-price segment requires a completely different pace of development. Time to market is just two years. In the premium class we test a lot. Summer conditions, winter conditions, and so on. In low-price vehicle development there is no time for so much testing, even though no compromises can be made on quality. It must be absolutely clear from the start what engineering functions you are to provide, and in what way you are to provide them. Because you don't have time to do two or three years of testing. The thing has to fit, and it has to work. And that's that.

How do you help advance innovation?

Well, as CEO, it is my job to create the right framework, the right mindset. I have to make sure the financial resources are there, and that they are there consistently. Priorities are set by the board of management, and above all by my deputy, Dr. Siegfried Dais, who is responsible for the R&D of the Bosch Group. As CEO I make it clear to everyone that innovation is a top priority by making it a key message in our communication. These are the main areas where I can influence the company as concerns innovation.

How do you organize your R&D efforts?

As I mentioned, the board decides what the strategic areas of our work will be. We consider mega trends and the major technological developments we see on the horizon. As to our R&D operations themselves, here we have different levels. We have several hundred associates working in corporate research. They pursue really basic research— research which is not so much linked to the existing products of the company. Instead, it is linked to fields we think the company should be active in 10, 15, or 20 years from now. Most of these fields are concerned with the issue of energy sources. What kind of innovation do we need if we want to secure energy supplies in the future? These researchers are given pretty much a free hand to go about their work as they see fit.

On another level, senior management in the divisions define what the next generation of our products will be, and the one after that. We always try to think in three generations. We have a current generation in production, the next one in development, and the third one on the drawing board. These third-generation projects, which are given high priority, are financed partly by the divisions and partly by corporate HQ. They are managed jointly by my deputy Dr. Dais and the president of corporate research. Here, corporate research staff and people from the divisions work together in a network. At the same time, the divisions develop the platforms for the next generation and prepare their start of production.

Could you give me an example of your role in advancing innovative product developments?

Let me give you two examples. Number one: Before I was CEO, I worked in the Diesel Systems division. During my time there, in the mid-1990s, we introduced diesel direct injection systems. I wasn't directly involved in any development work, but I had to make sure that this product would be a market success. So we needed a lot of process innovation, and I was involved in building up an appropriate business unit. Today diesel passenger cars have a market share of more than 50 percent in Europe, and I am proud of having been part of that success story. In the meantime Diesel Systems is our largest division, with annual sales of €9 billion. In a way, it's a large company of its own within Bosch.

Number two: As CEO I take a personal interest in the development of micro-electro-mechanical sensors (MEMS). We are the world's leading producer of these sensors. You need them for ABS, for ESP®, and for airbags, for example. Without them, these systems would not work. Now, some time ago we decided to enter the consumer goods segment. This is quite a challenge for an automotive supplier. Why? Because the speed of development is totally different. A car generation lasts around three, four, five, six years. In consumer goods, a generation is over after three, four, five, six months. If you miss your cue, you're out of the business.

But there were two reasons we took this step: first, the business is attractive, and second, it is an area to which we can apply our know-how. The sensors we produce are essential components of products such as cell phones and laptops. At the same time, we learned how to speed up our development processes, which in turn benefits our automotive business. By the way, nearly all the MEMS producers around the world use a manufacturing process called the "Bosch process." The two Bosch associates who invented it received the European Inventor of the Year Award 2007 from the European Commission and the European Patent Agency.

How do you reward innovative performance?

There are several ways in which we do this. We have a standard improvement process in which all associates can participate. This is an important source of ideas for improvement, especially in the manufacturing area, and we are very successful there. Suitable rewards take various forms. Or again, we filed more than 3,000 patent applications last year. That's 14 each working day. The associates who come up with inventions that are successful in the market receive a financial reward in the form of inventor's compensation, which can be considerable. There's nothing wrong with that, since both sides benefit, the company and the inventor.

I would like to ask about future innovation. You already mentioned you are doing research in energy. How do you foresee innovations changing in your industry over the next five years?

Let me take the example of the automotive sector. There are still a lot of innovations that can be made in the classic internal-combustion engine: development there is not over yet. All this will improve the fuel efficiency of these engines in the years to come. We will see gasoline and diesel using combustion processes that combine the benefits of both approaches. Even now, pollutant emissions are low compared with the beginning of the 1990s. We have reduced them by more than 90 percent in that time, but we haven't finished yet. Diesel will remain the most efficient engine for long rides. But there will also be a lot of research on the hybrid. In big cities, with their stop-and-go traffic, hybrids allow braking energy to be recuperated and overall engine efficiency to be enhanced. So parcel delivery companies such as UPS will use hybrid technology. The third area is the fuel cell, which could also be a solution for the mega cities. At the moment, there is still no infrastructure for hydrogen. But such an infrastructure could be set up in the mega cities. And the fourth direction is the electric car. The development of batteries is progressing fast. Bosch has signed a joint research agreement with BASF, Evonik, and some other technology companies to develop the next generation of lithium-ion battery technology, and the one after that.

What are some possible future changes to Bosch's approach to innovation?

I mentioned our commitment to continuous improvement. This commitment means we are constantly changing. In the future, more of our work will be done in research networks with other companies. In the past, Bosch generally tried to develop everything on its own or in joint projects with our customers. But we have not worked very often with other companies, or with competitors. Now that we are faced with such enormous challenges as climate change or the need for energy, I believe that we will be working more and more in research networks together with other companies. Such challenges require a concerted effort.

There are also many areas of research which could be important for the company, but we cannot develop everything on our own. Nor can we keep track of all the development work being undertaken around the world. What we need, then, is a kind of interface to research clusters that are working on areas which are interesting for us. This is why we set up the Bosch Venture Capital Fund last year, to which we committed €200 million. Nobody knows today what this money will achieve. It may be that the €200 million are lost. This is a new way of thinking for our company.

Is it also a major step that you might have to cooperate more than in the past with research institutes, universities?

We do that already on a large scale. But the idea of cooperating with other companies that might also be your competitors later on is new. Other companies have no problem with such ventures. They set them up without delay, and later on they also share the work of manufacturing. But this is not the typical way Bosch does things, not the "Bosch DNA." Changing this will require a major paradigm shift.

What are some limits to innovation?

In the automotive sector, quality and reliability standards clearly limit the speed of the innovation process. There is absolutely no way we can make compromises on this point. Sometimes innovations take a very long time. Take the electronic stability program, for example. It took us 15 years to develop ESP®. In 2007, the FIA (Federation Internationale de l'Automobile) gave ESP® its award for road safety. This is gratifying recognition of the enormous amount of effort we invested in its development. We worked on diesel direct injection for over 20 years, accumulating heavy losses before we earned our first profit. For a publicly traded company, such an investment would be unthinkable. Under the pressure of shareholders, Bosch would hardly have had the time to turn diesel technology into the success story we see on the roads today in Western Europe.

But on the other hand, and this is the interesting point, we also produce consumer goods in our company. For example, the Ixo: By the end of 2007 we will have manufactured 8 million of them. It is the widest selling hand-held power tool ever made. We developed this tool in a mere 12 months. And the key to its success is its lithium-ion battery. Bosch was involved in battery technology in the past, but left the business in the 1980s. At that time, however, our R&D was already working on lithium-ion technology, which was then applied to power tools. So a new product can take 20 years or just 12 months.

As global markets become ever more important, do you foresee any changes to Bosch's business priorities?

Automotive will clearly be the main focus of the company. But we are trying to create a better balance among our three business sectors. We have our Automotive Technology business sector, our Consumer Goods and Building Technology business sector, and our Industrial Technology business sector, which is mainly Bosch Rexroth and packaging technology. But we are also considering a fourth sector, which at the moment goes by the mysterious name "UBX." We see this as a melting pot for long-term ideas. Most likely it will include some energy ideas, such as renewables. We can find some new opportunities for our micro-mechanical semiconductor competence in there too. Just talking about UBX has generated so much long-term thinking in the organization that we now have more ideas on the table than we can handle. And now the ball is back in our court; we have to decide in which fields we will spend our money. But as a long-term target, I predict that UBX will generate sales worth several billion euros by 2015.

I think you also have to learn cultural change. One of our values is cultural diversity. We have to be open to this if we want to be really successful and grow internationally. After all, our future growth will be in the emerging markets. We devote a lot of effort to cultural training before we send Germans on assignments outside the country, and before non-Germans come to us. How does a German work, what makes him tick? How does he think? Why is he so direct? Why is the chap in China not so direct? We also try to give all our associates intercultural training in such matters.

I will give you a specific example. We have a management partnership with Denso, one of our main competitors in the market. It is the world's second largest automotive supplier. We form a group made up of six junior managers from each company, working on long-term issues related to the automotive industry in general. This is basically a way of learning more about how the Japanese think and operate, and how they look at things. This is very important as we progress toward international networks.

Do you have any advice for other CEOs who are trying to improve innovative performance?

It's not for me to tell them what to do. We all have to find for ourselves the solutions that are right for our companies.

HENNING KAGERMANN

CO-CEO

SAP AG

SAP is the world's largest provider of business software, delivering products and services that help accelerate business innovation for its customers. Today, more than 46,100 customers in more than 120 countries run SAP applications. SAP solution portfolios support the unique business processes of more than 25 industries, including high tech, retail, financial services, healthcare, and the public sector. Founded in 1972 and headquartered in Walldorf, Germany, SAP has leveraged its prominent position in enterprise resource planning software to expand into related markets, such as supply chain management, customer relationship management (CRM), and business intelligence. SAP currently employs more than 43,800 people in more than 50 countries worldwide. The company has a global network of 13 research and 9 development centers. In 2007, SAP invested €1.46 billion in research, representing 14.3 percent of sales.

BIOGRAPHY

Henning Kagermann is Co-CEO of SAP AG, a role he has shared with co-CEO Léo Apotheker since April 2008. Together with Hasso Plattner, co-founder of SAP, he was co-CEO from 1998 to 2003, and sole CEO following the election of Plattner as chairman of the SAP Supervisory Board in May 2003.

Kagermann joined SAP in 1982 and was initially responsible for product development in the areas of cost accounting and controlling. He subsequently oversaw development of all administrative solutions, including human resources, as well as industry-specific developments for banking, insurance, the public sector, and healthcare. His responsibilities also included finance and administration, as well as managing all SAP regions. Kagermann has been a member of the SAP Executive Board since 1991.

Kagermann studied physics in Brunswick and Munich, earning a doctorate degree in theoretical physics in 1975 from the Technical University of Brunswick, Germany, where he was promoted to professor in 1985. He taught physics and computer science at the Technical University of Brunswick and University of Mannheim, in Germany, from 1980–92. Kagermann also received an honorary doctorate from the University of Magdeburg, Germany, and was a trustee of the Technical University of Munich from 2001 to 2007. He is also a member of the honorary senate of the Lindau Foundation for Nobel Prize Winners Meetings.

Kagermann is a member of the supervisory boards of Deutsche Bank AG, Münchener Rückversicherungs-Gesellschaft AG (Munich Re), and Nokia.

INTERVIEW

What are the major reasons for SAP's innovative performance?
If you are a world market leader like SAP in a very dynamic high-tech industry, it's obvious you must be an innovator. You can choose to be a fast follower, and for one or two products, I think this was the case for SAP in the past couple of years. But in the IT industry, you can't be a fast follower

in too many cases; you must always try to stay ahead of the competition. It's not like in other industries where you can say: Others are innovating, I'm copying. That's not possible for us. As number one in a very innovative industry, with a big gap between us and the number two, we can't just follow the rest of the market, we have to be a leader in the industry, and—together with partners—we set the trends that others will follow. In many cases, you can't buy it, so you have to innovate yourself. If you are the market leader, your customers expect this. Innovation is key to our success.

Do you use your global reach for stimulating and developing innovative products?

The critical piece for us is our portfolio. We have always more ideas and opportunities than we can actually deliver to the market. So, we have to educate our people that it's not about having even more ideas, but about picking the right ones and bringing them to the customer as part of an optimized portfolio. Innovation is more than just ideas, it's ideas brought successfully to the market.

Therefore the question is: Where do you get the information required to put a successful portfolio together? I think we are making headway here. We have the Industry Value Networks, with leading partners and customers, industry-specific large global enterprises, typically 10 to 15 leaders. We invite them and speak with them about their industry. So, we get a good perspective on what's happening in this industry.

Another source is definitely our field organization. They meet a lot of clients, and our colleagues from portfolio management interview those in the field and collect information on what our customers expect, what they need to be even more successful. This is not as systematic as the first source, but it gives you a broader picture of the industry, especially if you have such a strong customer base as SAP does among the leading companies in every industry. Then we have our strategy group, they watch the market, the competitive landscape, and focus on what we have to do in order to stay competitive. And the same happens from the technological side, where our tech guys in the Office of the Chief Technology Officer (CTO) and SAP Research identify future technologies the market may not yet be aware of. Here our technology partners play an important role; we speak, for example, regularly with Intel to understand what the next wave in processor technology is.

So this all comes together, and we get enough information across all regions and all industries. The difficulty is to make the right bets. You have to find the right balance between short-term indicators like customer feedback, and long-term indicators like trends discussed in our Industry Value Networks or future technological standards and architectures. At the end, we look to our portfolio and decide how much we want to spend to keep it innovative and ahead of competition. The process is not too difficult, but you need a lot of experience to make the right decisions. *You talked about partnering with competitors. How do you define the line between partnering and protecting your knowledge?*
We have learned that sharing knowledge is the best way to get knowledge. If you feel you have to protect yourself, you have already lost half of the game. The point is to be faster than the others through openness and sharing. You must have enough capabilities to get enough benefit out of it. Then normally it's a win–win. There are only a few situations where you need IP protection. This happens if you develop something jointly, or if the other party is a big player as well.

We make IP deals, for example, with Microsoft and IBM, before we enter co-innovation. But with smaller partners, and we have a lot of them, it's not necessary, there is always a fair trade-off. There are very rare cases where clients believe something was relevant to IP, but that can be handled. In the end, I would say that our co-innovation is 90 percent based on openness and sharing, and 10 percent needs IP protection.

Does India or China play a role in your business?

Both countries are increasingly important markets for SAP. And we always try to have some development facilities in our relevant markets, so that we can be closer to our customers. But one has to be careful, as every country is different. In India, for example, people are more disposed to get all they can from your company, then go out to the street and find a competitor. But we take the risk, and have built a strong development unit in India. China is a little more difficult; at the time being it's hard to find applicants with the right skills for deep development, so we go more for support functions. In the long term, that situation is going to improve in China as well.

What are the main challenges at SAP with regards to innovation?

The challenge is to keep the balance between the cool ideas you need to appeal to people, and the power to bring these ideas at the end to the market in a way our customers expect from us, which means with high quality, high perform-ance, high stability, and all this brought easily to scale. We experience this challenge whenever we make a small acqui-sition: You bring in entrepreneurship, people with cool ideas, a cool demo that convinces a few, but later on, when it comes to delivery, these products don't have the depth and the quality people expect from SAP in many cases. So, you have to find a way to keep this entrepreneurship alive, but on the other hand, you must make people aware that they are no longer in a start-up company. You need this entrepreneurship at the beginning, you don't want to leverage the big engine of SAP too early, because this will kill entrepreneurship; but you do want to leverage it early enough, because otherwise you will kill your reputation in the market. That's the biggest challenge, because it's about different cultures. We now try to protect entrepreneurship in kind of an incubator status until the "big machine" takes over. Maybe we should have done this earlier, like other large companies have done. But that is something you learn time after time, when your company has grown over decades at such an amazing speed.

What are the limits to the pace of innovation?

For a market leader like SAP, the limit is we cannot do things "quick and dirty." This is not meant to be pejorative here, it's just that smaller companies can bring innovations to the market in a way that SAP cannot afford in terms of customer expectations. For a start-up in the Silicon Valley, it's enough to have an English version that works fine in the United States. Nobody expects more from them. If SAP comes up with the same innovation, the expectation is much higher: full integration, localization across the globe, etc. And that will take more time, more engineering. So, we have the advantage of a good brand name, but this can become a disadvantage if our logo is on a solution that does not completely meet our standards. In many cases, testing our market with a quick solution is not possible. Sometimes you find clients who are willing to say, OK, it's just a test. But in most cases, they would not engage if we say it's just a test. Our clients engage because they know we have a track record to make it happen later on, and make it happen in our industry means to have it 10, 15 years in the market. So what can be a reasonable innovation from a small vendor's perspective may be no more than prototyping for us. And our challenge is to choose those innovations that will bring long-term benefit to our customers.

How do you organize innovation?

Let's focus on product innovation in particular, because most of SAP's innovation is product innovation. We do business model innovation and process innovation as well, but in the end, we are still by far a product innovation company with roughly 12,000 developers. So we have a large organization where you expect that the products coming out will be successful in the market. Organized innovation means first of all to organize this large number of people, coordinate the teams across the globe, etc.

And then we need two things to ensure it's not just an inside-out product piece. One is the portfolio management already mentioned. At the end, this is decided by the SAP Executive Board and then cascaded through the organization. Our Board members have no silo mentality, and whenever we talk about innovation, it's not just about making a product, but how can we make an idea become a product that will be a success in the market. If we bring key innovations to the market, like our SAP NetWeaver technology platform or recently our new midmarket solution SAP Business ByDesign, we have CEO Councils to manage the value chain across the company. It's a holistic approach to innovation, so that at a certain point in time, we have everything aligned: product development, support, field, sales, consulting, and partner organization. Otherwise, the final product is there and the field wouldn't know about it, and no support and no training would be prepared.

For smaller innovations, we use a ramp-up approach. We test the market with defined customers, we accompany the customer very carefully, and development is involved. The product is not yet generally available, and we can still delay delivery. The ramp-up typically involves 50 to 100 clients, assigned by the field, and we have certain rules like that 50 percent of the consulting is done by SAP in these cases to ensure an efficient learning curve. We monitor the process, what the response is, how good the quality is, etc. And then we say: OK, let's make it available to everybody.

You will have noticed I talked less about the invention itself, but much more about engaging the organization. The reason is that I believe this is still the bigger piece of the challenge. For SAP, the difficulty about innovation is not so much to have the ideas, because we're not doing science, but business. And our business is not to have a product that works for a couple of clients only. We have to bring ideas to scale. In our industry, what's worse than having no clients is having one client. Because you have to treat that client well, and in the end, the product gets quite expensive for yourself. If you want to run a profitable business, you have to select your innovations very carefully. That's why you have to engage the whole organization.

What are the challenges in product innovation?

Two things are key to product innovation: One is to listen to the customer, and the second is not to listen to the customer. If you only listen to the customer, you will never make the really good stuff. If you never listen to the customer, you may not survive. So, you have to listen and select between what's really needed and what customers just believe they need. This is a pretty tricky thing in standard software. You shouldn't take the word of a customer as dictated requirements. For individual software, that's OK, because it's what you get paid for. But for standard software, the biggest challenge is to filter ideas and do innovation in a way that you can scale later on. And no customer can give you exactly the requirements for a standard product that will sell on a large scale.

Why can't you continue to rely on product innovation only?

You can change the game of an industry with a revolutionary product, the famous "killer app," or you change the game with a different business model. Compared with product innovation in the software industry, the business model is pretty old-fashioned, the way you buy, install, implement, train, and upgrade software. I think even as a very successful product innovator, you should ask yourself whether your future couldn't be a combination of a new product with a different business model, because that could really change the game. But don't get me wrong, I am not talking about changing a business model without touching the product.

With our new midmarket solution, we decided to innovate our business model. We are building a parallel business to what we have, by entering a new market with a combination of innovative product plus process plus monetization. This is not easy, and it's interesting to see that the market gives us credit as a product innovator, but now that we are innovating the business model, people are skeptical and say we have never done this.

But it's important that a company learns this as well and sticks to its strategy; because I think you cannot be just a product innovator forever.

In this case, we identified "software as a service" as a model for the future. Not the only model, but an important one. It's an opportunity to serve more customers with a standardized solution at lower cost. And in homage to the traditional "innovator's dilemma" by Clayton Christensen (if you want to do something entirely disruptive, do you wait until somebody else does it, or do you do it yourself?), we decided to do it ourselves. But you cannot do this with your installed base, because they are used to the established business model and you cannot take a risk that ruins your success. So, you have to select a customer group that is untapped, which we did, and do it entirely different. That's the only way to do it. And if you are successful, you can come back to the installed base. With a strong customer base, balancing an old and a new business model is a nice challenge.

What is your role in encouraging innovation?

One of my functions includes responsibility for a big piece of development, but that may not be typical for a CEO. More generally, what a CEO obviously does is to start from a strategic point of view. Our strategy, which is normally defined for five to seven years, is not only based on what we want to be in the world, namely the market leader in enterprise software, but also around products and innovation. Five years ago, for example, we decided to bet on service-oriented architecture (SOA) with an ambitious enterprise SOA approach. This was a big shift that impacted the entire company, and now we can say we've been successful in doing so. That's what I would call a strategy, not just "we want to be twice as large as today." The strategy has to address the "how." Not with every detail, but including some directions on innovation, be it product or process or business model innovation. And as CEO, I always felt it's good if you can explain your product strategy, its architecture, and why you are doing things, on a high level to financial analysts and business analysts. So, you start making strategic assumptions about markets and technologies, and the direction you want to go in. You write this down, and then you make your bets. You start cascading it with a four, five, and six- year perspective. Now you have a very big frame, and you cannot escape. That's the first thing.

The second is to execute, which is sometimes even more difficult. You must deliver on the street's expectation short term and stay on track for your long-term goals. Whatever you do on a shorter time scale, you have to make sure it fits at least 80 percent into the bigger strategic frame. I admit that there may be certain years where you have to adapt your strategy, the market is very turbulent. But if you want to kick off the next wave, you have to think pretty long term in our industry. And once you have decided, you have to fight it through. Otherwise, you will lose your credibility. I will not say that we have never failed, but we never leave a market. Either we come up with a successor product or find another solution to satisfy our customers' needs. I cannot remember having a solution that failed and as a consequence, we left that market.

How do you compensate and reward innovation?

Across the organization, those who are involved in innovation normally have a personal target plus a team target. Sometimes it's only a team target, and for higher positions it's the team target plus a company target. So, the more responsibility you have, the more your incentive is linked to the success of the entire company. This means you avoid a battle between "silo-ed" innovations. That would be something SAP cannot afford, as our success is based on integration. So, helping other groups is very important, and we try not to focus too much on individual targets because of this integration. We always believe it's not one person; it's more a team that leads to success.

Do you think you as a CEO have an influence on the culture of innovation at SAP?

Yes, and as a CEO you send signals even if you don't want to. I refer very often to customers, to our reputation of making success happen for our customers. This sends a signal in terms of quality, reliability, engagement, and so on. I could deliver different speeches, and tell stories about the guy who wakes up at night and comes up with this brilliant idea that helps him build a company from scratch, right out of his garage. That would send a different signal. But I believe we are now in a position where the other signal is more important. I could also spend a lot more of my time in our labs and enjoy watching the next cool stuff emerge. Our large installed base is a great asset, and spending more time with your clients, listening to them, and getting their feedback is stimulating. The question is where your priorities are: my priorities are quality and customer satisfaction.

Have there been recent changes to SAP's innovation strategy?

I think we have done a good job engaging customers and partners in our communities of innovations, like the Industry Value Networks. But we have to further leverage our research. The link between research and development will improve, and we will better leverage the innovation potential in our academic network with hundreds of universities.

We have strengthened our portfolio management, as I felt it was being triggered too much from the bottom up. We have reduced the complexity, because we have a lot of products, and we had to reduce the complexity for our clients and for ourselves. We have to be clearer in terms of what's coming next.

How do you foresee innovation changing the IT industry?

I see two trends that impact the way you have to bring innovation to the market. The first is a variation in the requested speed of innovation. On the one hand, globalization has enormously accelerated the pace of business, you have to act very quickly to keep your competitive advantage. On the other hand, enterprises on a certain level are getting a little bit more conservative. Investments are so huge that

CEOs ask for long-term engagements, like a marriage. So, therefore the question is: how can we satisfy both requirements? How can we enable our customers to innovate at the speed of their business? Different industries have different speeds of innovation; some are more conservative than others. And, in each business, there are different speeds of innovation; we have core processes that need to keep the lights on all the time, where people do not want much innovation but stability and no disruption. But at the same time, they want innovation where they can differentiate themselves against the competition. This typically happens more at the edge of the business. As a software vendor, if you want to deliver solutions for the entire company, you have to define the right architecture that allows you to enable these different speeds. Keeping the big piece stable and nevertheless innovating around it is not that easy. We have found a good way, which I believe is so far unique in our industry, to handle this and satisfy both requirements.

The second trend is somehow related to the first one; it's the fact that the consumer is gaining more influence even in the enterprise. The consumer of enterprise software is someone in the organization, but the customer is the management, the CEO, CFO, or CIO. You have to deliver on your customers' expectations, offer higher productivity through standardized and more automated processes, and at the same time, please users with easy-to-use solutions that can be personalized and help them doing their job. That's not an easy task, as the consumer space is moving very fast, with shorter product life cycles. So-called "business users" want to have the newest stuff at work as well, they want tiny little tools that can be bought with cash in their pockets. You can allow people to work with such tools and establish kind of a shadow IT. But you can imagine it doesn't really help corporate IT on a mid- to long-term scale, because you increase complexity and risk supportability and compliance. At the end, the company will turn to its standard enterprise software vendor and say, please help us integrate everything. So, in order to avoid this up front, our challenge is to improve the convenience and the experience for both, the customer and the user. That's the difference between our case and a consumer electronics company where the customer and user are identical.

Do you change innovation policies in a recession?

We had this situation in the IT industry in 2001, 2002. It's natural that in such times you become more focused on the short term because you have to bring yourself back into a position where you can act more forward-looking and strategically. If times really get tough and you think too much in the long term, missing the results, and severely losing valuation, you might not survive. So, there is a point in time when you have to be more short-term driven. But whenever you realize you are through the worst, I would say go as fast as possible back to innovation, hopefully faster than others.

Therefore, good portfolio management is so important. It allows you to change the mix of those things that have short-term revenue impact and those that have long-term impact on our strategic market position. That's the flexibility you need to steer an innovative company through the ups and downs of your industry.

What advice can you give other CEOs to improve innovative performance?

I've never seen a company other than SAP from the inside. Every industry and every company is different, so I can only share my experiences and then let others decide whether and what to learn from it. Because I know this culture, I know these people. An innovation strategy cannot be imposed from the top down. You have to do it with the people you have, you have to do it in the framework you have. So, I can explain what we are doing and why, but I would not give general advice on how to innovate. If someone asked me for advice regarding IT, then that is different. If someone comes and says, I have this IT project, what should I do? then I can answer—it's my profession.

OLLI-PEKKA KALLASVUO

PRESIDENT, CEO AND GROUP EXECUTIVE BOARD CHAIRMAN

NOKIA

Nokia, the world's largest manufacturer of mobile devices, is at the forefront of the convergence of mobile devices and the Internet. Recognizing the rapidly expanding opportunities to offer enhanced capabilities to consumers and enterprises, in January, 2008, Nokia reorganized into three major units, Devices, Services & Software, and Markets, to apply its manufacturing and marketing prowess to delivering new, content-rich services together with devices. The company also supplies equipment and services for fixed and mobile networks through Nokia Siemens Networks. Headquartered in Espoo, Finland, and founded in 1865 as a Finnish wood pulp company, the company entered the telecommunications equipment business in 1960. Nokia has a strong R&D presence in ten countries and in 2007 the company invested €5.6 billion in R&D, representing 11.1 percent of net sales. Among numerous innovations, Nokia introduced the first fully digital local European telephone exchange in 1982, and nine years later, a Nokia phone placed the world's first GSM call over a Nokia-built Finnish network. Today, Nokia develops new technologies and services to offer mobile access to the Internet.

BIOGRAPHY

Olli-Pekka Kallasvuo has been President and Chief Executive Officer of Nokia since June 1, 2006. Olli-Pekka joined Nokia in 1980 as Corporate Counsel, and has held roles of increasing responsibility since that time. In 1987 he was appointed Assistant Vice President, Legal Department, and in 1988 he was named Assistant Vice President, Finance. In 1990 he was promoted to Senior Vice President, Finance.

In 1992, Olli-Pekka was named Executive Vice President and Chief Financial Officer. In 1997–98 he served as Corporate Executive Vice President, Nokia Americas, being responsible for all Nokia's business operations in the Americas. He returned to the position of Chief Financial Officer at the beginning of 1999, the position he held prior to moving to the United States. From 2004–05 Olli-Pekka was Executive Vice President and General Manager of Mobile Phones. On October 1, 2005 he was named President and COO before his current appointment as CEO.

Olli-Pekka has been a member of the Group Executive Board of Nokia since 1990. On April 1, 2007, he was appointed Chairman of the Board of Nokia Siemens Networks, and nominated as member of the Board of Directors of Nokia in May 2007. He also serves on the Board of EMC Corporation.

He holds a Master's degree in law from the University of Helsinki. Prior to joining Nokia, Olli-Pekka held various positions with the Union Bank of Finland. He was born in Lavia, Finland. In his spare time, he enjoys golf, tennis, and reading about political history.

INTERVIEW

How do you encourage innovation at Nokia?
On one hand we invest a lot of money in R&D. It is true that

the more money you invest, the more innovation you get. On the other hand, innovation also requires perspiration as well, it requires a lot of hard work.

The culture also needs to support innovation. Of our four core values at Nokia, one is a Passion for Innovation. That's very much highlighted in communications with employees, we discuss the values frequently with our people. In that way we live our dreams under that value, a Passion for Innovation.

One needs to remember that innovation does not happen in technology alone. It happens in all areas of business. We invest a lot of money in marketing, adding a lot of value in marketing the brand. Innovation happens there as well. Looking at technology alone is far too limiting. Business model innovation is becoming more and more important. When the business environment gets more complex, you can really face difficulties positioning yourself because the competition is very often new, industries do converge, and you have to navigate with how your business models evolve. A lot of innovation is needed in that area as well, and I think business model innovation is something that needs focus as well. It does not happen automatically.

A good example is the Nokia Research Center, which has traditionally been doing technology innovation, the "R" part of R&D. We have now assigned them responsibility also to innovate business models and how technologies and business models link, and have an impact on each other. I think this has been very energizing for that team of people who previously have been looking just at technologies. Now they are seeing the business model at the same time as they are making technology innovation. That has been a very, very positive experience. So innovation needs to happen in all areas where the company is active. It very often relates to quality too. Quality affects everything we do, improving quality means doing things better and you need innovation in order to keep being able to do things better. So in that way innovation is a very broad concept.

What innovation policies do you pursue?

I feel it's very important that innovation is not owned by an individual or just a few units in a corporation, but it is something that everyone needs to feel responsible for. If we need to improve what we are doing, then we all need to innovate.

Although we are now an incumbent, for a long time we were a challenger, a small company attacking the incumbents. I think the challenger mentality continues to be very much here at Nokia. We do understand that when you are a challenger you have to go for it, as opposed to defend. And that challenger culture, freedom to fail, so to speak, is there very much in the company. We accept that when you have to go for it, you sometimes fail. Failing in defending is sometimes more difficult because you are supposed to win if you defend. A small company soul in a big corporate body, I think is a very important aspect, and that's something we try to nurture and maintain very much. That's one of my biggest tasks, not to let the incumbency creep in, in terms of us becoming defensive. It's very important.

What do you see as a major innovation challenge for your company?

It's the risk than comes with being an established incumbent, the risk of becoming complacent.

How important is off-shoring and outsourcing?

If you are a global company and you have operations everywhere, the whole concept of off-shoring becomes irrelevant. For us there is no such thing. I have been talking about this to some companies who are using the term. You are making a mistake if you look at it in this way. There is no off-shoring, you're just present in different places. It is easy for us because in Finland we don't have a large home market, so we have operated on a global scale for many years, it's really second nature to us.

But outsourcing we do a lot. That you need to do extensively and that's always a big challenge. For big companies, outsourcing might be as a concept a bit like "I move this piece for somebody else to do." That might be easy. But partnering sometimes is difficult because it's more than that, and in that way challenges remain for every big company because there's so much knowledge and skills in the company that it's easy to start thinking we do have enough, although we don't have enough in terms of skills and capabilities. That's something one needs to drive quite a lot.

As an example, we do have a Corporate Alliances Board that is led by a senior member of the team that is basically there to make sure that we have enough focus on partnering, because partnering is so important when it comes to innovation. Partnering in the real sense of the word is definitely one of our focus areas.

We partner a lot with academia and we have chosen some universities globally that we are focusing on. Stanford, MIT, Cambridge, Beijing and others get extra attention so that we can really make sure that the partnering happens extensively there. Some focus is also needed here. You cannot say you partner with just anybody. We have made clear choices and that has proven to be important.

Do China or India play a role in your innovation strategy?
One can pick China and India when it comes to your global presence and use them as examples, but they are just examples, in the same way as talking about off-shoring. But we have been focusing quite a lot there. The thinking here is that we must integrate these countries to our innovation network

on an equal basis, as opposed to being subordinated in some way. Because it's so important that people in all countries, all areas, have meaningful assignments, as opposed to being subordinated somehow in terms of the skills that are required or in terms of the totality of what you are doing. The thinking is we don't outsource internally less important tasks to India, for example, because that's not motivating, that's not good for the totality, it's very much on equal terms. If you do that, I think the results are much better.

We do have 7,000 people in China doing R&D and I always say that in China we want to be Chinese. We don't want to be a Finnish company who's active in China. We want to be in China as Chinese. I have spoken about this often with the Chinese authorities and they really appreciate this concept, because many other companies work with a different mindset, saying these are our Chinese operations. I'm saying this is Nokia in China and it's Chinese. The experience we have gotten in China and India, as just two examples, has been very, very good.

I'll add this, although it goes beyond the theme of innovation. We have put the head office of a global unit in India, the services unit within Nokia Siemens Networks. So the guy who's running that has global responsibility for that business, but the unit is based in India. This is extremely energizing to the teams in India because they see they are an equal part of the total, as opposed to subordinated in some way. It's very, very important.

We also extended our internal venturing fund activity to China early on, so it was not that we started somewhere and people traveled to see if there are opportunities in China. We have put up these operations there as well, again approaching China on equal terms, as opposed to subordinated or being in sequence. This is very important too.

We are doing things now in India that we were doing in China four or five years ago. That relates to the development in the marketplace and where India is now in comparison to China, so there's a time lag. So we are not as big in India as in China. Our biggest market is China, our second biggest market India, then the United States and the UK. When you are in that situation obviously you are looking at these in a very different way in comparison to a situation when they would be number nine and ten on the list.

Now that Nokia is a global company, do you still conduct R&D in Finland?

We do have quite a lot of R&D activity still in Finland, and it's interesting that Finland has been able to maintain quite a good position when it comes to basic R&D, especially in the area of radio technologies. It's kind of difficult to explain, but I think it has to do with accumulated skills, almost like tacit skills, because of the history, so in that way we have a big population doing R&D still in Finland and the output is good when it comes to efficiency, so in that way they have been performing. But of course the emphasis has been shifting.

Have there been changes to innovation policies?

One thing that has changed is we have become more active when it comes to acquisitions and acquiring skills, capabilities, technologies, markets, I think that relates to the fact that there is this convergence of mobility and the Internet that is happening as we speak. The competitive environment is changing. We definitely don't have all the technologies, all the software we need. After a lot of soul searching we have gone into acquiring companies on a pretty targeted basis. That has definitely changed and that, of course, will add to the diversity, which is extremely good, and in that way foster innovation.

Diversity is really a key word when it comes to innovation, in my mind. And the positive friction that you get from diversity is extremely important. Teams that don't have diversity innovate less in my opinion. That is why we are really focusing on diversity at Nokia. We are following that, we are setting targets and planning quite a lot how we can increase our diversity.

It continues to be a challenge to have enough Asian diversity. If you look at the management teams and the other teams, we need to increase Asian representation in the teams. I think this is both a big challenge and great opportunity for many Western companies.

Have there been recent changes to how you approach innovation?
No, I don't think we have changed in that way, it's really very clearly the way we have been working. I very much believe this old saying, "if it ain't broke, don't fix it" is wrong! You need to fix things before they get broken in business. In that way, you evolve taking baby steps all the time. From a mindset point of view that's always difficult, and this relates very much to innovation because organizations tend to say, "Hey, why the change? This works." Then you have to say, "But we need to change proactively before things get broken, and in that way evolve." And very often in business, if you have to make a really big change, you have typically failed to make small changes often enough. In that way I believe very much in evolution, as opposed to revolution in making things happen. This challenging and questioning the current paradigm is always so important. But that you need to nurture and it isn't easy for big companies.

What is your role as a CEO in nurturing these changes?
I need to be the main guy when it comes to pushing this "it ain't broken, but we fix it" thinking. And of course sometimes it's very exciting and energizing for the organization

140

because change is that as well. But then again, resistance is always there. Now as a company we are in a situation where we are changing quite a bit. Because what we are saying now is mobile devices are not enough any more from a consumer point of view and we are basically saying that the hardware and the simple communications functionality is not enough, but consumers want to buy solutions. So they want to buy a music solution. Communications device, of course yes, because we all use voice communications, but it might be a music device as well. So it's a solution and we need to be able to combine devices more like hardware with services in order to sell solutions, and this is a big change. And this is what we are driving right now. It relates to the fact that the Internet and mobility are converging. Here there is so much room for innovation when it comes to ways of working, to business models, and to technologies.

As very often with innovation, it can be scary, but in spite of that you need to have focus and choose, and very often this choosing is quite difficult. So how do you choose what is the innovation you drive? It's quite interesting. Even when it comes to business models I sometimes wonder how many business models can you really can run in the same company. Because if you get too diversified when it comes to your business models, you easily don't have enough focus.

What is your overall role as CEO?

The role of the CEO very often is simply to be a change agent, that's very clear. And then one needs to be head of the personnel in the company, that's what I feel like that's my role, I allocate a lot of time for those two tasks.

Who are the innovation decision makers?

As I said, I don't think any one individual can own innovation, so in that way it's really pushing a lot of people to act.

I would say here there's a big difference between different types of companies. If the company is capital intense, where really it's the capital that is working, you invest in a big factory, it's a really, really important decision, and it happens at the Board, and then you put in the capital, then the rest is more about execution. You make sure that it works and you have to innovate there. But it's a different type of situation in comparison with a company that is people intense, where really your factories are the people working in the company, as opposed to heavy capital investment. In a company like that, communications are even more important than in a capital-intense company, because there are thousands of people making decisions on a daily basis and one must make sure that the decisions they are making are more or less aligned. They cannot be fully aligned, that's the whole point. But they should be pretty well aligned and that's why communications about the direction and what is happening in the company, and discussing and getting and giving the feedback, are so, so important. The communications part of managing is much more important in a people-intense company.

We have done quite a lot here, in fact. We came up with new Nokia values in the spring of 2007. We really involved personnel there to the extent that in fact they made the decisions, which was very interesting. So we had global café sessions where 2,500 people participated in different parts of the world for two days to discuss what are the Nokia values, how should we work together? And then they sent their representatives to a local event in Helsinki, where there were 150 people, fine-tuning and streamlining, discussing, coming up with ideas and concluding that these are our values, this is how we work together, and so forth. I went there on the afternoon of the second day, and my mindset was that I had come to accept or approve or disapprove, because I have to like these values too. And there were other members of the senior management there too, probably with the same mindset. When I saw the tidal wave that came up, that had generated a lot of power all over the world, that these people were representing, they were so excited that I noted that even if I wanted to, I could not say no. Fortunately I did like the outcome, but that's not really the point! So in that way, much of the change was generated by the people themselves. And then thereafter we ran a 72-hour continuous Nokia Internet jam where basically 13,000 Nokia people participated to discuss the values and how we should work based on them and what should we do in our business, and what our direction should be. It was very, very useful in three ways.

First, it definitely fosters innovation, because here people can learn about what other people in the company feel, what should we go for, and what are the key priorities, and what are the key ideas as well. It's great, and this is the second aspect, because it's so energizing for people because they feel that they can be part of something, and really have an impact. [*TR* – *It's an incentive?*] Yes, it's an incentive and it was really taken in that way.

And the third aspect, of course, is that during the jam also the management can communicate direction, that is also important in order to keep making the alignment continue in the decision making. So in that way I would say innovation needs to be everywhere, not isolated somehow in terms of how money is being used and so forth. In fact, the money that is being used, the money that is needed, that allocation, happens in the normal course of planning in different units. In that way it's very much an integrated activity we have here.

We, of course, do have innovation activities, innovation champions. We are running innovation fairs that communicate and foster innovation on a general basis. But it is not isolating when it comes to the thinking.

The Innovation Summit, we do that as an interactive approach for business, product, or project idea generation. So we bring together technology and business executives. We have been doing this since 2003. Each event brings together 40 to 50 nominated experts and innovators with technology and business backgrounds, outside and internal. We really concentrate on what is happening in this field. We have done this in entry products, for exploding markets; that was the theme in 2003, we have succeeded quite well by the way in those markets, maybe partly because of this. Other Summits have covered imaging, smartphone, wearable electronics, mobile services, and opportunities in a converged world, and we organize two or three of these innovation summits annually. But this is more like fostering innovation, as opposed to owning it. As I said, business model innovation must be part of that.

What do you think are the challenges with regards to innovation in the next five years?

I think the challenges here are the complexities of the business and the business environment we are living in. We are now seeing a situation where many our competitors are new entrants. Think about the fact that we have become the biggest camera manufacturer in the world. Last year we manufactured 200 million cameras. They were, of course, in a communications device, but they start to become so high-end that we are competing with the camera industry. So Canon is clearly a competitor, in a major way. Now take music devices as another example. We are the biggest music device manufacturer in the world. Last year we sold more than 140 million music devices, hence Apple and Sony are also our competitors.

Then other people are entering our business using different business models. Apple with the iPhone, RIM with an e-mail-based solution, but they are selling a lot of devices. Microsoft with their operating system and so forth, so the complexity here is changing quite a bit, and as I said earlier, we are now combining devices with services on top to sell solutions. And that's a big, big challenge, and in that area we will compete against many of the Internet service providers and that's new competition again for us. The challenge here is, of course, the fact that complexity of the business environment, or the business we are in, is changing dramatically and that's a big innovation challenge.

I see that to be relevant in a couple of ways. One is the fact that when it comes to dynamics, the consumer electronics or hardware business that we have been in, mobile devices includes software, but we sell it together with the hardware. The business dynamics in a consumer electronics-type hardware business on one hand, and then the Internet services business on the other hand, they are completely different.

In the Internet world it's the beta culture. You fail fast. Basically you go ahead, if you fail, you change direction, and it's very much a faster cycle than in a hardware business where quality requirements are something completely different and so forth. The innovation challenge, on the one hand, is how to combine the two in the same company; that's a big and interesting challenge.

Does that mean you have to organize innovation in a different way?

No, I don't think it will mean that. But it will mean that we will reorganize as of January 1, 2008, we will have the devices business, the services business and then we go to market together selling solutions. Because my thinking is that you can't isolate innovation. We simply are saying that innovation in the devices part, we need to continue, but at the same time we need to innovate when it comes to the services part, and we need to innovate how we combine the two to form a solution. That's a big challenge, and when it comes to what we are doing about that, we are acquiring companies, as I said, adding skills, diversity that is needed, and we have been doing quite a lot of job rotation, as well as hiring quite a lot of external talent as well. Again in order to bring in the diversity.

But I would say the innovation challenge here will change a bit, not only because of the complexity, but because I think more and more business model innovation will become important. There we have, like I have said earlier and this is very, very important in this context, we have given our research units business model innovation tasks as well. So it's not the technology alone.

We need to look from the very first beginning how to monetize that, and how to make that happen, because you can choose between so many different models now in a digitized world where all the information is digital. So there are a lot of possibilities to choose, what should be our business model here. I think there's more challenge there and more needs to be done. I have been discussing this quite a lot with Henning Kagermann, CEO of SAP, for instance, and I'm sure he will talk quite a lot about that when you meet him. This definitely is one area that I think is increasingly important. Partly because of the fact that the world is changing and becoming more complex, and I think he is experiencing exactly the same with SAP.

Are there changes to innovation policies during a recession?

In a recession it's of course what you can afford when it

comes to spending your money, but other than that I don't think it has an impact. You need to innovate, and act, and work exactly in the same way. When it comes to money, of course you need to invest as much as you can, but that's basically happening in every situation. You are investing what you can, but that's only part of it.

How do you foresee innovation changing over the next five years?
Patience is needed as well when it comes to innovation. This is very, very, very difficult very often. So how do you have enough patience to wait that something really becomes meaningful, as opposed to killing something too soon? There is no perfect timeline. Very often I'm seeing that here we have innovation, a business prospect, or something that might pay off in three or four years' time. I'm thinking, three or four years, that's a long time. But then I turn my mind back in time, three or four years, and I realize that was yesterday. It goes so quickly in business, but the concept of time is a bit different depending whether you look ahead or back in time. I very often do this test with myself, and I say, OK, in three or four years, but that's very soon in fact. That test very often helps to say, OK, that's good, it will happen soon, in fact, and it's not that long a time. So that patience with innovation, that's very, very important. Because things do not happen overnight, there is not that magic bullet that will change everything overnight. But in the current world it's more and more difficult to have this medium-term thinking, or that's even a long term, three or four years in business now.

I really believe that people need to understand when you are changing something or renewing something, that it's not saying that the old was bad. The old was good at the time it was put in. But as environments change, competition changes, what was right three or four years ago might

147

be outdated now. And then you have to renew. The thing that is new now will be old in three or four years' time. And in that way it's an evolution, and when you are stopping doing something, when you are saying this is not good any more, you are not criticizing anything. But many people feel now we are saying, they have difficulty coping with the fact that something needs to be stopped in order to make room for something new. This is extremely important in the area of innovation. Because typically if you have to start something, you have to stop something as well. Because you cannot continue to add, add, add layers of activities and overhead, and that type of renewal is extremely important when it comes to innovation.

Do you think because of convergence, Nokia and other companies will have to partner more?

Absolutely. In comparison to ten or even five years ago, partnering has increased multifold, and even in the way you partner and compete with the same companies. We see that extensively now and you need to be able manage that as well.

Where is the line between partnering and sharing knowledge, and competing?

It's very often very difficult and very sensitive, and every major company needs to deal with that topic or matter going forward. Every major company needs to do that. The complexity here is very energizing.

What advice can you give other CEOs to improve innovation?

I would say this is a very difficult area, so innovation is difficult. I say that it's perspiration and innovation in the way that it's not one great idea that will make the day. In business this Holy Grail is not found very often, and in that way you need a lot of focus, you need a lot of activity, in fact you need a lot of money as well. That's the reality.

The other item that I would highlight is the importance of culture. When it comes to culture, I would take up two items. One is you can fail, that's not punished (unless you keep making the same mistake!). And two, external orientation is so important when it comes to innovation. Big companies so easily become internally driven. And very often when you get internally focused, you lack the diversity as well, which is so important because that positive friction, like I said, is extremely important.

ARTHUR D. LEVINSON, Ph.D.
CHAIRMAN AND CEO
GENENTECH

Genentech ranks among the world's leading biotechnology companies, developing innovative therapies to address significant unmet medical needs. Launching the biotechnology industry with its founding in 1976, Genentech manufactures and commercializes multiple products for serious or life-threatening medical conditions in the fields of oncology, immunology, disorders of tissue growth and repair, neurobiology and infectious disease. The company currently has more than 100 projects in its pipeline. R&D expenditures were $2.4 billion in 2007, representing 21 percent of revenues. Research activities are conducted at its South San Francisco corporate headquarters. Genentech's medical and scientific achievements include a history of "firsts" for patients. Among them are:

- *the first human protein (somatostatin) produced in a microorganism*
- *the first recombinant DNA drug marketed (human insulin)*
- *the first laboratory production of Factor VIII, a clotting factor for bleeding in hemophiliacs*
- *the first recombinant DNA product manufactured and marketed by a biotechnology company, Protropin (somatrem for injection) growth hormone for children with growth hormone deficiency*

- *the first FDA-approved therapeutic antibody for cancer, Rituxan (Rituximab)*
- *the first FDA-approved therapeutic antibody targeted to a cancer-related molecular market, Herceptin (Trastuzumab)*
- *the first FDA-approved anti-angiogenic cancer therapy, Avastin (bevacizumab).*

BIOGRAPHY

Arthur D. Levinson became chief executive officer of Genentech in July 1995. Dr. Levinson was appointed a member of the board of directors that same year and named chairman of the board in 1999.

Dr. Levinson joined the company in 1980 as a senior scientist and subsequently held the position of staff scientist and director of Cell Genetics at Genentech. He became vice president of Research Technology in 1989, vice president of Research in 1990, senior vice president of Research in 1992, and senior vice president of Research and Development in 1993. He has been a member of Genentech's executive committee since 1990. Prior to his employment with Genentech, Levinson was a postdoctoral fellow in the department of microbiology at the University of California, San Francisco.

During his career, Dr. Levinson has served on the editorial boards of Molecular Biology and Medicine, Molecular and Cellular Biology, Journal of Virology, *and* Virology. *He also served on the boards of the Pharmaceutical Research and Manufacturers of America, the Biotechnology Industry Organization, and the California Healthcare Institute. Dr. Levinson has authored or co-authored more than 80 scientific articles and has been a named inventor on 11 United States patents, including inventions in the research of production of recombinant proteins.*

Dr. Levinson sits on the board of scientific consultants for the

Memorial Sloan-Kettering Cancer Center and is a member of the advisory councils for the California Institute for Quantitative Biomedical Research (QB3), the Princeton University Department of Molecular Biology, and the Lewis-Sigler Institute for Integrative Genomics, also at Princeton. He also serves on the board of the Technology Network.

Dr. Levinson serves on the corporate boards of Apple Inc. and Google Inc.

He received the Irvington Institute's 1999 Corporate Leadership Award in Science and was honored the same year with the Corporate Leadership Award from the National Breast Cancer Coalition. He was inducted into the Biotech Hall of Fame at the 2003 Biotech Meeting of chief executive officers. BusinessWeek *named Levinson one of the Best Managers of the Year in 2004 and 2005, and* Institutional Investor *named him America's Best CEO in the biotech category four years in a row (2004–07). In 2006, Princeton University awarded Levinson the James Madison Medal for a distinguished career in scientific research and in biotechnology. Also in 2006, Barron's recognized Levinson as one of the "The World's Most Respected CEOs," and the Best Practice Institute placed Levinson on the "25 Top CEOs" list.*

INTERVIEW

What are the major reasons for Genentech's innovative performance?

Luck. That doesn't sell books, does it? But that's part of it, always. I think it would be interesting, though, when you look at companies that are considered to be "innovative"—such an overused word I'm getting tired of it—but you have all these companies trying to do great things. Then every once in a while something emerges and everybody says oh, there must be some tremendous kind of brilliance, culture, or environment, how can we all emulate this and copy it so we're going to be innovative and successful? I think a lot of it has to do with randomness. I think a culture can squash innovation, but you can't start with a bunch of people and say, all right we're going to do A, B, C, D, and E, and wonderful things will necessarily come out of that. The best thing you can do, at least in part, is to make sure that you eliminate obstacles to creativity and innovation. We try to do that at Genentech.

As we've grown from 100 people to 1,000 people to approximately 11,000 people, we hear more and more concerns that we are doing things that might get in the way of creativity, for example bureaucracy and slow decision making, and employees find that their work feels more cumbersome. So we've worked hard to keep things simple. But keeping things simple doesn't necessarily mean that you're going to do wonderful things. It means that if things are extremely complicated and slow and bureaucratic, and if someone does have a good idea, you're likely to miss it. I think part of this is making sure that you do things that don't get in the way of people. Clearly, from the very beginning here, we have pushed down decision making and we've made sure that when we hire really great people that they have—and I'm talking now about the R&D side in particular—the responsibility and accountability to do the science.

It's very much not a traditional type of a model, where there's some guru up here with a bunch of minions, then more and more minions, and the guru gets the credit for everything, which I don't like. We just make sure that we bring in the people and they get the credit and they make the decisions on how to proceed. The role of the top managers here really is to set a general direction but their responsibility pretty much stops there. What gets done, and how it gets done, is decided by individual scientists and clinicians.

What are the major innovation challenges?

There are a lot of them. We certainly have been successful, in part, because we never accept the status quo, we never accept conventional thinking, conventional wisdom. When you look at the points in the history of our company where we have made the biggest difference, in almost every case it was where everybody, almost all the experts, thought that we were doing something stupid. We encourage clear thinking and we try hard to avoid the herd mentality. If you look at what's going on in the pharmaceutical industry right now, you have almost every company chasing the top five "obvious things." There are certain things that are likely to represent promising targets, but if you have 30 good companies all chasing a few things, then somebody's going to win, but your odds are pretty low. So we really prefer looking elsewhere for the most part. Added to that, people's thoughts on targets and technologies, in my view, are often wrong.

In the case of the pharmaceutical industry, it's interesting to me how top-down driven the decision-making process is, and in the case of science, how most of these top-down decisions are made by non-scientists. How on earth do they have a clue figuring out what is promising or what is not promising? They don't, so they typically latch onto the conventional wisdom, and they'll say OK, we're going to do this, but there's no value-add there, absolutely none. It's just derivative kind of work, that will tend to be either copying people, or catching people, or chasing people, and I think in the long run that's not a sound approach.

How do you avoid the herd mentality?

We try to hire people who are clear, independent thinkers and who are not afraid to challenge conventional wisdom.

Let's go back in time 20 years. Genentech is known now as a wonderful monoclonal antibody company, that's part of what we do, it's a big portion of our business. Monoclonal antibodies are large molecular weight molecules that your body makes to fight infections and can target certain foreign pathogens. In the mid-1980s, everybody thought this was going to be fantastic, so everybody was doing monoclonal antibodies and for about five or seven years none of them worked, absolutely none of them worked. It got to the point where everybody thought that they would never work. So almost everybody abandoned them. But the reason they didn't work in the 1980s was because everybody was using antibodies that were derived from a mouse. And when you inject a mouse protein into a human, the human rejects it because it's foreign. So this wasn't a good test. All these mouse antibodies were failing and people thought monoclonal antibodies didn't work and most companies stopped working on them. Well, what didn't work was the fact that you were injecting a mouse rather than a human protein.

Now that's not rocket science, this is really kind of basic stuff. But it just illustrates the example that I talked about earlier where you get people making decisions who in many cases don't know much about the science. So hundreds of companies were trying to make monoclonal antibodies and none of them worked. All these clinical trials being done with the FDA's blessing were failing. At Genentech, we put all of our energies into making human monoclonal antibodies. Of course we had great success. That was the time when everybody was fleeing from the approach.

Let me give you another example. You know about the blockbuster model of the pharmaceutical industry. Now, it takes about a billion dollars to develop a drug, and there's no point, according to this big pharma model, in developing a drug that doesn't have blockbuster potential, because otherwise you'll invest a billion dollars, you won't get sufficient revenues and you will lose money. That's part of the reason everybody is going after the few kinds of obvious blockbuster-type products. About 10 or 15 years ago we were working on an approach for women with breast cancer and we identified a target that we thought could be attacked with a monoclonal antibody that might help women with breast cancer. It looked like only about 25 percent of women with breast cancer had the genetic problem that this antibody would attack. So we said, OK, 25 percent, that is still a lot of women who are dying. About 180,000 new cases of breast cancer are diagnosed every year just in this country and about a quarter of them had the genetic lesion that we were attacking, and the big pharma model said, don't develop it because you're throwing away three-quarters of the market, it won't be successful. We decided to move forward and were commercially successful at developing a drug called Herceptin that can significantly prolong survival in this patient subset, and the product had over $3 billion in global sales last year.

We fundamentally believe that if we have a drug that works, it will make money. But most importantly, it will help patients if it works. And furthermore, we don't want to treat the three-quarters of patients who won't benefit from the drug. I don't want to sell a drug to somebody when I know up front they're not going to benefit. There's very little work being done in the industry to figure out which patients won't respond to which drugs but it's the right method for us. Part of what I think has accounted for our success is that we really try to take the long view. I'm far more interested in what's going to happen seven years down the road than what happens tomorrow.

What are some advantages of the longer-term view?

When you take the long view, the business decisions can become very different—when you say "How am I going to maximize things eight years down the road?" rather than next quarter or next year. You always need to do what's right in any event, but there's almost never a tension between what's right and what's good for an individual or a company ten years down the road. It's interesting how that works out. In general, companies are reluctant to take the long-term perspective. There's a lot of pressure on Wall Street to deliver performance next quarter or next year, and companies tend not to place an appropriate emphasis on what's right seven years or ten years down the road.

Is global reach important for you?

Absolutely. There's a lot of brainpower and talent and great technology outside the United States, there's no doubt about that, in Europe, in Japan, and increasingly in China. So being able to tap into the intellectual capabilities of people all over the world is essential. We are primarily a US-based operation. We have global partners, first and foremost Roche, and Roche has rights to our ex-US markets, and sometimes they exercise these rights and sometimes they don't. When they don't, to this point we've always worked with other companies, and we have not developed any broad commercial presence outside the United States. And I don't see us doing that any time soon. But in terms of the R&D efforts, we're accessing talent everywhere.

Have you ever considered creating other R&D locations?

We have always rejected a dispersion of our R&D efforts. We believe there's a tremendous value having all the leaders be within a ten-minute walk of each other. So the scientist can talk to the intellectual property lawyer, who can talk to the clinician. Everyone then attends the same meetings and decision-making sessions. And again, this is in contrast with most of the pharmaceutical industry, where you'll have research institutes all around the world. In many cases, these are historical accidents because they acquired a remotely located company for a legitimate reason, and they have people there and they end up with people all over the world and they're flying on jets much of the time just to talk and meet. We actively reject that approach.

There are people who think that we should open up an office in Seattle, North Carolina, Texas, or Ireland. So far, obviously, we've resisted that. If we were to open up another research office, we would do it very carefully, and probably in the context of a whole new therapeutic area rather than splitting oncology in half, and having half of it be 3,000 miles away, and half of it here. And if we did open another research office, we would want to replicate the kind of company and culture that we are somewhere else. But again, I'm not seeing a big need to do that. There are disadvantages of keeping it centralized. Probably first and foremost, the Bay Area is an expensive place to do business. Land is expensive and housing costs are expensive, so we don't always end up recruiting everybody we want just because of that. But at the same time, if we were to be located in Texas, let's say, some people wouldn't want to live in Texas.

What is your role to advance innovation?
It's really setting a tone for people. I don't really do much more than set a tone. But I like to set a tone where people question authority, where they challenge, question everything. I try to make sure that the people we hire have the right motivations and intentions. Typically when we've

made a big hiring mistake, it's not because the person lacks intelligence, or is not a good person, they're just used to a very different environment. If the first question out of their mouth is how much money am I going to make or how many stock options do I get, they're probably not the right person for Genentech. Of course we want to reward people for being successful and doing well, but that should be third or fourth on their list of priorities. We want to bring in people here who want to make a difference, who are really committed to making great new drugs and are passionate about it and are willing to work really hard to do it. We have a set of core values, and we want to bring in people who find some resonance with these core values. We don't want to bring in people who might be wonderful for another drug company, but not fit here very well. I don't want to say we're better than other companies—we just are who we are and it works for us. The alignment between what our values are and what a person's motivations might be is critical.

How do you decide which developments to pursue?

We have groups and committees that make decisions. We try hard to make sure most people on these committees have a scientific or clinical perspective so that people who are making the decisions understand what the heck they're deciding. I've already touched on that, but I just want to make sure that when we make decisions they're good decisions, and you can't make good decisions if you don't really understand what you're being asked to decide at a very deep and profound level. Beyond that, as I said, we want to bring in people here, even junior people, who have the ability to take their work in the directions that they think make most sense, consistent with the general directions set forth by our company's leaders. So we have a big effort in oncology and immunology, and we're not in reproductive health, for example. We wouldn't want to bring in someone and say you're your own person and do what you want, and have them start working on drugs in the area of reproductive health. There are rules, but once you say "I'm going to work on cancer," you're pretty much free to do whatever you want to do.

How do you reward innovative performance?

I'm a big fan of rewarding people who have made really important contributions. So if somebody comes up with a major drug for cancer, for example, then we want to make sure that person is rewarded with financial incentives for doing great work. We have a well-balanced compensation profile right now where we look at salaries, we look at bonuses, and we look at stock options or equity positions in the company, and we try to structure this in a way that will keep us competitive from a salary point of view, from a bonus point of view, so that our employees are generously compensated, commensurate with our performance. The last ten years have been really great for us performance-wise, so we want to make sure employees are recognized with very good bonuses, and on the equity front, if somebody is a top performer, that they're recognized by good stock option grants. And, again, that's different from most other companies in the pharmaceutical industry, where in general, the stock options go to a small handful of people. Here, virtually all employees get stock options and about 80 percent of the stock options are given to non-officers. If you go to the annual reports and look at the big drug companies, you can see what percent of the options are given to the officers of the company. Then look at ours. It's very different.

Do you believe you might have to change your innovation strategy in the next 5 or even 15 years?

I would say not in any obvious way. Things could change,

but we've had a good track record over the last 10 or 15 years coming up with innovative products and medicines. The pipeline looks really interesting and promising to all of us. If all of a sudden something changes and there's a big dry spell, then I think we all scratch our heads and ask what's going on here. But we don't think that's likely, though it's never impossible. So no, I think we're on a pretty solid footing here. *How do you foresee innovations changing Genentech over the next five years?*

It's always hard to predict. Five years is close enough that I don't think there's any general theme here that will kick into play. For example, will there be a whole new technology that will revolutionize medicines in the next five years? No, I don't think so, but it could happen. I think over the next five years there could be new technologies that might start surfacing as likely candidates to change things. For example, there could be new delivery systems for drugs, new forms of small molecules that are based on a different chemistry. These are all possibilities, but I think that a five-year time frame horizon is too small to see it fundamentally changing things.

I think what you will see, and continue to see, is that individual medicines and drugs will be successful, that will come out of creative, innovative thinking. Historically, most of that thinking comes from academia and the drug companies wait and watch, and when they see something—usually after it becomes relatively obvious—they'll say, here's a target some academic identified, so let's start cranking away at it. What we like to do here is be part of that basic discovery process. We therefore strive to hire scientists of the caliber that can compete with the scientists at Harvard, MIT, Stanford, and CalTech. We do that. In fact, we recruit pretty heavily from those types of institutions.

There are two reasons for this. One is that we can, by doing so, hire much better people, because the best people want the opportunity to do the groundbreaking research, they don't want to be simply told, look here's a target, make 8,000 molecular derivatives of this starting chemical and see which one binds the tightest. That's nice and really important, but you tend not to have the smartest people getting excited about doing only that. They want to contribute to the breakthrough science. You bring in these really, really smart people to do that, and it has all kind of benefits for the whole company. It's very difficult for scientists to get promoted here without a great publication record, so we celebrate publications, and share the results within the academic and scientific community.

But the other thing is if we have these smart people and are involved at the basic research level in terms of contributions, then we believe, and I think experience has taught us this is correct, that we'll be better able to understand and assess possible breakthroughs or possible new research, we'll be able to understand the significance of it six months or a year or three years more quickly than somebody who's not really deeply involved in the science. We're not going to wait until *Science* magazine, or the *Wall Street Journal*, says this is really important. By that point, you're way too late. So by bringing in these smart people it gives us a head start. But you can't bring in the great people without letting them do and contribute to the basic research.

What aspects of the business are likely to see the most changes?
Again that's hard to say; there are possibilities all over the place, certainly in the science, in the small molecules, in the drug delivery area, even in manufacturing where we're really pushing a lot of limits on yields, trying to get these biological processes to produce higher levels of proteins.

There are some really interesting technologies coming into play there. There is also a lot of discussion, understandably, about the cost of healthcare in this country, in fact around the world, and about the ability to deliver good quality healthcare that is perceived to have some type of value, more so than it does today. I think in the sales and marketing area there could be some real opportunities for innovation too. Because at some point the healthcare expenditures in even first world countries will hit a wall. I think the industry has to be as much a part of that solution as the government and we hope we're not going to be found to be in a completely reactive position to the insurance companies or the government. I think we have to take a leading role here and so far I've not seen a lot of signs of the industry doing that.

If there is an economic recession, do you change anything with regards to innovation?

No, if anything, it reinforces the importance of innovation. There are good times and tough times. If we find ourselves in tough times, and I'm speaking theoretically because we've had the luxury of having 10, 12, 15 pretty good years, R&D won't be first on the chopping block because we will pay the price of that over the long run. Now part and parcel of that is we really try to send out this long-term message to our investors. We don't do this in a vacuum and we certainly rely on the support of the investment community here, but I think any even semi-sophisticated investor knows how we manage the company. We really strive for investors who are investing for the long term, not because sales next quarter might beat estimates by 11 million dollars. We are looking for investors who are focused on sustained long-term performance that beats the market over five or eight years, not one or two quarters. I think most of our investors are pretty sophisticated, and they would be disappointed with us if the first thing we did in tough times was to chop R&D because that's not why they're in the stock.

Now that Genentech is a big company, will it be difficult to keep Genentech different from the other large drug companies?

That's a good question. I would say so far not. People said big drug companies aren't very efficient, and that's true. But small ones aren't either. And they always leave that half out. So if you always talk about the first half, you think there's something wrong with being big. But if you look at the whole equation, you see the big ones aren't efficient and the little ones aren't either. Now there are exceptions, but there are exceptions on both sides, and it seems to me we're a much stronger company today than we were ten years ago precisely because we're bigger. We have tremendous infrastructure, we have great support for so many of the efforts that we are engaged in that size is a strength for us, and I think size should be a strength for most companies. Things get in the way of that, but everything else being equal, I would much rather embark on a new era with 11,000 employees and the kind of company we are today, than with 1,000 employees or 2,000 employees that we had ten years ago.

We've had a good run. It's interesting between Amgen and us, we account for about two-thirds of the profits of all 1,400 biotech companies. It really makes my point that most of the big companies are not very successful, and most of the little companies aren't very successful either. Nobody ever mentions that.

Almost no biotech companies make money. There's never been a year in the history of the biotech industry where the industry as a whole has made money. Every single year the industry as a whole has lost money. Last year it lost $3.5 billion. You read all these analyst reports and for the last 15 years they always say in two years we project it will change, the industry will become profitable. It never has been profitable. That doesn't mean it never will be, but here we are 30 years later, not one profitable year. This field has been the biggest money-losing enterprise, I think, in the history of mankind. That's why I'm humble enough to know that luck has to play a little bit of a role here. I don't think that we're so wonderful and so terrific that there are only two companies out of 1,400 because we're so brilliant and smart. We're all rolling the dice a little bit here.

We're pretty good at what we do and so there are certainly watch-outs, and it relates back to decision making, bureaucracy, and accountability that I referred to at the beginning about being big, but those aren't impossible situations. You can deal with those and I think we are dealing with them really pretty well. I would much rather be a big company than a little company if I had to compete, and we all have to compete. As an old timer, I was hired here when we had fewer than 100 people, and I remember when we got to 500. People said, "Oh, we're so big now, how are we going to keep the culture?" All right, well we did. People asked the same question when we were 1,000 people, 2,000, now we're over 10,000. I'm used to that. I've heard it for 25 years and we've done just fine. Again, just to come back to the point, I would much rather compete with our 11,000 people than with 1,000 people.

Do China or India play any role in your strategy?
Right now China and India are areas on the radar screen that will probably have the biggest impact in the area of generic drugs. They're very interested in developing medications that are based on existing novel medications

once the patents expire, and they can take advantage of their low-cost labor force. They develop factories and manufacturing capabilities that will allow them to really quite inexpensively replicate the medicines coming out of Germany, the UK, and the US, the novel drugs. But patents expire, appropriately so, and society needs access to low-cost drugs and it could well be that China and India are going to be two dominating forces in the generics industry, and that's fine. But that might have a big impact on some companies. I think maybe it will be less so for us because we constantly focus on, our mission, is to develop break-through drugs and novel drugs that will make a big differ-ence in patients' lives. After we get our 17- or 20-year run, we're perfectly happy to say, OK, somebody else can now take it, from there on, that drug. If we can't continually come up with new, better, greater drugs, then we shouldn't be rewarded. The competition on that front doesn't make me nervous at all. I think it's the right thing for society.

How do you share information with partners, academia, and other industry researchers?

If you have a collaborator on a given drug I think both sides recognize that it's essential to exchange information. I think more broadly, companies tend to be closed and secretive, and very few companies take the approach that we do of publish-ing their work. Many companies won't publish at all. But if we make a great drug, a great discovery, we can't wait to publish it, relying on the patent system to work, which it generally does quite well. We're not nervous about that.

There's always a trade-off, it's never perfect one way or the other. But you have to ask yourself, are you better off in the long run to publish quickly, let's say, or to never publish? Those are two extremes. Certainly sometimes when we publish breakthrough work we will engender competition and we'll get other people excited, and in a narrow sense you could say that's a disadvantage because we might have lost n months of lead time. But the benefits of that, in my mind, just far outweigh the disadvantages. I'm not saying there are no disadvantages, but it nets out as a positive and we always try to think in large, broad terms and look at the net benefit. It's so easy to get caught up in this negative and that negative, and then say, OK, we're not going to do this any more. Then you don't think about anything you're losing by that decision.

It's interesting, one of the things that happens, at least in the drug industry, is that all companies think they have more interesting things than they can develop. But very few large companies will ever out-license something. To me it's a fascinating psychological exercise. Why is that? I think the answer is obvious, although sad. Few CEOs or leadership teams like to out-license an internal product, only to have a partner make it a success, because that tells you, look how stupid you were. But far better to allow the external opportunity for development and get 12 percent royalties, and have society benefit from that medicine, then to say, I'm not going to let them have it because what if it works? They all want to in-license, but who wants to out-license? The people that are out-licensing are the little start-ups. The big drug companies, who should have a thousand times more interesting things to out-license, almost never do it. Something's wrong with that.

Do you think there will be more partnering between large drug and biotech companies over the next five years?

I'm not sticking my neck out with that prediction; most people are predicting that. The pipelines are lean at most big pharma companies, so they're looking to the biotech world for new, interesting ideas. So yes, that will continue.

It's interesting, if you look at the number of new molecules in 2004 that were approved by the FDA, it was the first time more new molecules came out of the biotech companies than out of big pharma. So that really says that the world is changing, that biotech's presence is real, and not only growing, but it's a serious presence.

How will the biotech industry change and what will be the CEO role to make biotech companies successful?

My answer should be, I would expect the same answer of any biotech CEO, it's all going to depend on the pipeline, and the ability of the researchers' drugs, to get through Phase I, Phase II, Phase III clinical trials and end up with medicines that will really make a difference to patients. If a company does R&D well, that company will likely do well as a business. If a company doesn't do R&D well, they're likely to fail. Execution is important, you have to manufacture, commercialize, you have to do all that stuff well. But in the final analysis what really matters is the pipeline and the kind of drugs that you're putting through and that are going to come out of it. So that's why our relentless emphasis continues to be on research and development, the quality of the scientists and clinicians, and the quality of the decisions that we make at each step in terms of whether we will go or not go with this drug or pathway. It all comes down to that. I just don't see that changing for many, many years.

Do you have any advice for other CEOs to improve innovative performance?

I'd tell them to ask somebody else, because they couldn't necessarily follow our rules in a culture that's very different. There would be a clash potentially. I'm not smart enough to figure out how some of these big drug companies that do not have a great innovative record, all of a sudden, snap your fingers and have them turn that around. I don't know what to say to them. It's a huge problem and you're probably familiar with all the statistics about how drug companies in the aggregate are spending a lot more money now on R&D and the output is only declining. If you look at the output by several metrics, probably most importantly by the number of approvals by the FDA in our country of new molecular entities, really novel drugs that are approved every year, they're pretty much declining for the last ten years, year by year, and the R&D expenditures are going up, up, and up. So there's a real problem for many companies, but it's not easy to fix without wholesale changes to the corporate culture, and few companies are willing to make that type of commitment and investment.

N. R. NARAYANA MURTHY

CHAIRMAN AND CHIEF MENTOR

INFOSYS TECHNOLOGIES LIMITED

Launched in 1981 by seven people with the equivalent of $250, Infosys is a leading global Information Technology (IT) consulting and software services company. Infosys designed and implemented the Global Delivery Model which set the foundation for IT services outsourcing from India. Offshore technology services let companies reduce the cost of IT infrastructure and related labor expenses, improve quality and innovation, improve the speed of delivery of technology solutions, and introduce more scheduling flexibility. Infosys's services today range across business and technology consulting, application services, systems integration, product engineering, custom software development, maintenance, re-engineering, independent testing and validation services, IT infrastructure services, and business process outsourcing. Infosys has R&D centers in six countries. In fiscal 2006, the company spent 102 Rs. Crore (1 Crore equals 10 million) on research and development, representing 1.13 percent of sales revenue.

BIOGRAPHY

Mr. N. R. Narayana Murthy is the Chairman of the Board and Chief Mentor of Infosys. He founded Infosys with six other software professionals and served as CEO for 21 years. Under his leadership, Infosys was listed on NASDAQ in 1999. He has also led key corporate governance initiatives in India.

Mr. Murthy is an IT advisor to several Asian countries. He serves as an independent director on the boards of several global companies including Unilever, London, and HSBC, London. He is also a member of the advisory boards and councils of several educational institutions including Wharton, Cornell, INSEAD, Stanford, Tokyo University, SMU—Singapore, Indian Institute of Information Technology—Bangalore (IIITB) and ESSEC, Paris.

Mr. Murthy is the recipient of numerous awards and honors. The Economist *ranked him eighth on its list of 15 most admired global leaders in 2005. He was ranked 28th among the world's most respected business leaders by the* Financial Times *in 2005. In 2004,* TIME *magazine identified him as one of ten global leaders who are helping shape the future of technology. He was featured in* BusinessWeek's *"The Stars of Asia" consecutively from 1998 to 2000. He was voted the "World Entrepreneur of the Year" by Ernst & Young in 2003 and as India's most powerful CEO for four consecutive years (2004 to 2007) by the* Economic Times. *He received the Ernst Weber Engineering Leadership medal from the Institute of Electrical and Electronics Engineers in 2007 for his pioneering role in the globalization of IT services.*

Mr. Murthy holds a B.E. (Electrical Engineering) from the University of Mysore (1967) and M. Tech. (Electrical Engineering) from the Indian Institute of Technology, Kanpur (1969). Honorary doctorate degrees have been conferred on him by leading universities across the world.

INTERVIEW

What are the major reasons for Infosys's innovative performance?
There are many, many reasons. First of all, as somebody said, necessity is the mother of invention. I believe that necessity is the mother of innovation too. In our case, when we started the company, we realized that India had considerable value to add to the global bazaar, and we wanted to develop a new software delivery model to improve cycle time, value for money, quality and productivity. When we first went to our prospects in the United States, they said, "Look, you are as different from us as day and night because, literally, when the United States wakes up, India goes to sleep and vice versa." So, we came back to India very disappointed. Then, we started thinking how we can convert what is apparently a big disadvantage into an advantage.

That is when we came out with the concept of the 24-hour workday. We went to our customers and said, "Look, we will combine your prime time in California with our prime time in India. So, when your people go home at 6 o'clock in the evening, mentally and physically tired, they can pass on the problems of the day to us in software maintenance and software development through electronic mailboxes. We will come to our offices bright and early at 7.30 in the morning. We will open our electronic mailboxes, look at those problems, and start solving them. By the time we go home at 6 o'clock or 6.30 in the evening, your people will be starting their work here in California. Thus, when your people are sleeping, we are actually solving the problems for you. Thus, by providing you a 24-hour work day, we are compressing the cycle time for solving your software problems." This is one good example of innovation.

Let me give you another example. Pretty early in our company's life, we realized that there was going to be tremendous opportunity for software development in the West, in general, and in the United States, in particular. We also realized that India had a huge English-speaking technical talent base in software. We wanted to leverage the power of the Indian talent to provide better value for money to our customers. So, we developed a software delivery model called the Global Delivery Model (GDM). In this model, we split a large project into two categories of activities. In the first category of activities, there is a high level of interaction with the customer, and, consequently, they have to be delivered at the customer's site (we call this onsite). On the other hand, the second category of activities has very little interaction with the customers. They can be developed away from the customer in scalable, talent-rich, process-driven, technology-based, cost-competitive development centers in countries like India. The customer gets better value for money because, in a typical project, only about 20 to 25 percent of the effort is added near the customer in the developed world, and 75 to 80 percent of the value is added from countries like India where the cost of software development is lower.

Second, using the huge supply of talent we have in India, we can quickly put together a large team to compress the cycle time for the customer. Third, because we have invested heavily in the software factories in countries like India, focused on training people, on quality, productivity tools, and technology, we provide a better quality of software to the customer. Just to give you an example, as against the then-prevailing 46 percent of projects being completed on time and within budget, today, at Infosys, 95 percent of our software projects are completed on time and within budget. So, this is another good example of innovation. As I said before, necessity is the mother of innovation. Because we wanted to leverage the power of India, and because the customers in the United States did not see how Indian companies could add value to them due to the enormous time zone differences and distances, we came up with these two innovations to convince our customers that we can indeed add significant value to them.

How important is outsourcing and working with external networks?

Working with other vendor partners is very important and relevant for our business. We work with several global corporations as our vendor partners in the United States and other countries. Generally, we bring partners to a project where we see complementary strengths in them. For example, we have worked with a consulting firm in the energy sector in the United States in a project on derivatives in the oil trade. We are experts in software engineering, whereas they are experts in oil derivatives and hedging. By combining strengths of our two companies, we could optimize the trading algorithms, the database structures and programs. We could enhance the speed of access to these databases and the user-friendliness of the user interfaces. So, leveraging the domain knowledge through outsourcing to consulting companies in specialized areas, I believe we can bring in tremendous sources of innovation to our customers.

What are the major innovation challenges at Infosys?

The biggest challenge to innovation at Infosys is ensuring that our people do not rest on their laurels. Our people have to realize that the rest of the world is moving faster, and faster. Innovation is necessary for us to be out in front of our competitors, differentiate ourselves from them, and add value to our customers. To do this, the best instrument is to proactively make our own innovations obsolete by widely disseminating them in the industry after we have taken initial advantage of them. For example, we have a very powerful platform called Influx. Influx provides us with tools to develop efficient and high-performance software systems with leading-edge architecture, design, and performance engineering models. After taking advantage of this tool for a year or so, we made it available to our customers, because we knew that this tool would get widely disseminated, and would thus create an incentive for our people to innovate further in this area.

The second challenge is fostering innovations in a large organization. As the organization becomes larger and larger, and as we focus on bigger and bigger initiatives, the new innovations get brushed away by the powerful, well-entrenched business ideas in the organization which bring huge revenues through well-proven innovations. It is a well-known fact that, in the beginning, the PC division did not get much encouragement in IBM because of the opposition from the powerful mainframe people. So, even at Infosys, we have to fight the vested interests and the powerful people who bring huge revenues using well-understood principles from killing small, innovative ideas, which will, perhaps, become huge revenue earners tomorrow. We solve this problem by allocating a certain percentage of the bonus of our senior leaders to both the number of innovative ideas they bring to the table each quarter and the revenue from those innovative ideas. So, we have created a financial incentive for the leaders of big groups to encourage innovation within their groups.

Could you give some more detail about how you measure innovation?
One of the key performance indicators is the revenue from new ideas, new services, new technology, and new business models. As I already explained, revenues from new ideas and innovations form a part of the bonus that we give to senior people. These innovations do not have to be the idea of the leaders. They could be from one or more of the thousands of people that work for them. We want our senior leaders to create an environment of friendliness, courtesy, encouragement, and helpful attitudes to these innovative ideas. They do not have to send us their ideas. We want them to implement those ideas themselves, enter new markets, derive revenues, and make profits. Otherwise, people will simply keep sending their ideas by e-mail and do nothing about it. Unless an idea is actually used, unless it adds value to the customer, and unless it generates higher revenues and profits than today, that idea or innovation has no value to Infosys.

What is your role advancing innovation?
At this point in time, I am the non-executive Chairman. I used to be the Executive Chairman of the company till August 2006. I am also the mentor for most innovations. I foster innovative ideas. I discuss with each business leader what good ideas they have and how they have converted them into revenues. In some sense, I am the elder statesman for innovation in the company.

Who has the responsibility to decide and implement innovative ideas?
At Infosys, by and large, responsibility for innovation is pervasive and goes down to as low a level as possible. The important thing is simply this. Our business is developing customized software solutions for the customer. As long as any of our people uses a new idea to reduce cost and cycle

time, or to improve productivity, quality, revenue per employee, profit per employee, or to enhance customer and employee satisfaction, we are happy. Because of such a model, the leaders of various units have created KPIs (Key Performance Indicators), for employees at every level of the organization.

What are examples of recent innovations and your role?

Well, for example, I have been working with the head of our Corporate Education and Research group on enhancing the quality of our internal faculty. We have designed a scheme to get professors from well-known universities throughout the world to hold a 20-day-long, 60-lecture, full-semester course in one month in leading-edge areas. Once we have ensured that this pilot is successful, we will roll it out to various engineering colleges in the country. Thus, it is likely to improve the teaching for students that we recruit. This will reduce the time we have to spend in internal training of the new engineers who join us. Thus, we improve the productivity of our employees to get better revenues.

I will give you another example in which I was not involved personally. It is about a company that sells stents. Stents are used in cardiac surgery and are very expensive. This company realized that the inventory management of these stents was not very good. They found that hospitals realize the lack of inventory of stents hours before they are needed in an operation. In some cases, they found an excess of inventory of stents. So, when the company approached us, we designed an inventory management system based on the use of RFID technology in the operating theater where the stents are generally kept. In the new system, when a stent is taken for an operation, the nurse will just scan it using an RFID scanner. This operation will automatically update the stents inventory in the operating theater of the relevant hospital and in the central database in the vendor company. Thus, the vendor has data on the real-time position of stent inventory and can replenish the stock with adequate lead time. As a result, we have made sure that every hospital has the required inventory of stents and that the cost of maintaining adequate inventory and the cost of lack of adequate inventory are both reduced. That is the way we brought the power of RFID to manage the inventory of high-value items in an operating theater.

Has this always been the culture?

We are a very young company; we are just 26 years old. Right from our beginning, we have had the culture of openness to new ideas, meritocracy, and excellence in execution.

What are the future areas of innovation at Infosys?

We have been bringing innovation in multiple dimensions. First, Infosys is becoming more and more of an end-to-end business solution provider, leveraging technology. That is, we are combining the power of our consulting group with our software development group and with our business process outsourcing group. In other words, we are creating seamless processes that take an idea from consulting to software development to business process outsourcing.

Second, we have come out with a concept called *Modular Global Sourcing*. That is, today, when you talk of outsourcing, generally, people think in terms of the vendor taking over the employees of the customer, and then running the data center, or running the operations center. We believe that this is not good because there is so much concern about creation and retention of jobs for the employees of the company. In our model, we do not take over the employees of the customer. We add value to the customer by taking over only a certain part of the entire chain of outsourcing in a modular fashion. For example, in some cases, we have taken over the entire software development part. In some other cases, we have taken over the entire infrastructure management. That is called modular outsourcing. I believe that this will become more and more popular.

The third area of innovation which we are working on is the Global Delivery Model for consulting. I talked about the Global Delivery Model (GDM) earlier. GDM is about splitting a large project into two categories of activities. One is heavy on customer interaction and consequently delivered at the customer site, and the other has very little interaction with the customer and is consequently delivered away from the customer site from countries like India. GDM was used primarily in software development. Right now, we have on the drawing board a plan to adapt the Global Delivery Model to consulting. For example, activities like preparation of the proposal, analysis, research, simulation, and modeling can be taken up in India while our consultants work with clients in San Francisco, New York, London, or Tokyo. In other words, 25 to 35 percent of the effort involved in a consulting effort can now be added from India. Thus, the customer pays less for this effort, and, in turn, gets better value for money. In addition, we can compress the cycle time by using the 24-hour-work-day concept. I believe there will be a greater and greater role for GDM in activities which hitherto were thought not amenable to remote value addition.

There is another innovation I want to talk about. It is our knowledge management system (KMS). In our business, productivity comes from reusability. In every project that I review, I ask two questions. First, how many of the reusable components that already exist on our knowledge management system did we use before actually starting a project, thereby reducing the work in that project? The second question that I ask them is how many artifacts, how many knowledge objects did we put back into the knowledge management system at the end of the project? Because, to us, it is extremely important to reuse knowledge, artifacts and objects that exist in our knowledge management system to improve our quality and productivity. This is another trend that will become more and more popular.

To create an incentive for people to add artifacts to our knowledge management system and to use artifacts in the knowledge management system, we have created the concept of a Knowledge Currency Unit (KCU). Basically, a KCU measures the reuse. Each time your colleagues use your reusable object in the KMS, you collect certain units of the KCU. The KCUs awarded for each usage are based on the number of function points of the code in the object as well as how often it has been reused. At the end of the year, let us say you have accumulated 1,000 KCUs. You can convert it into money. In other words, we have now created an incentive for people to put more and more objects into the system. It has been working for over ten years now.

The idea was developed by the current CEO of the company, Kris Gopalakrishnan. He was the Chief Technology Officer of the company when he developed this idea. It has been very successful. Thanks to such ideas, we have been winning the MAKE (Most Admired Knowledge Enterprise) award for several years now, including in 2007.

Let me talk about another idea that is still on the drawing boards in Infosys. This is a technical idea. This is called a collaborative, distributed software development model. Here, the challenge is to split a large software project into multiple streams so that one stream could be taken up in Frankfurt, another stream could be taken up in Bangalore, a third stream could be taken up in Sydney, Australia, and the fourth stream could be taken up in California. Such a development model enhances parallelization and reduces cycle time. For example, when our Sydney person goes home, the unfinished work comes to India. Our Indian professional starts adding value and he will pass it on to his Frankfurt counterpart at the end of his work-day. The Frankfurt person adds value and then he will pass it on to our California person. In other words, as the earth is revolving, you will see professionals from different parts of the world adding value, thus leveraging the power of a 24-hour day.

Do you cooperate with competitors?

We practice co-opetition: collaboration and competition. For example, we are working with Accenture in areas where their strengths are complementary to our strengths. In other areas, we are significant competitors. I believe collaboration will work only when the two partners bring complementary strengths to the table. As long as we can find complementary strengths with a competitor of ours, we are very happy to work with them in any project. For example, we work with another Indian company Wipro, even though we are a significant competitor of Wipro in software. Wipro produces computers and we install our banking software on Wipro computers, and together we service the requirements of banks in India and several parts of Asia. So that again is a co-opetition scenario.

What changes do you foresee for your business?

First of all, we will move more and more toward fixed-price projects because customers are sick and tired of consultants coming and billing them by the hour. So, there will be greater and greater pressure on all of us to submit fixed-price project proposals. Second, remember I talked about a collaborative, distributed model of software development.

Thanks to this model, there will be greater and greater focus on reducing the cycle time. Third, there will greater focus on leveraging the power of technology for improving the productivity of professionals. Fourth, evolving technologies like Web 2.0, on-demand services, on-demand software, and others which leverage the power of the Internet will help corporations considerably in creating a virtual company whereby company professionals from different parts of the world will work together to share ideas, to share knowledge, to reduce cost of operation, to improve quality, and to improve productivity for our customers.

Are there any changes to your innovation policies during a recession?

The mindset of innovation has to be constant in an organization. It is easy to create a sense of urgency during a recession because your sales are not growing, your margins are reducing and people have to make sacrifices. So, people understand the need for urgency easily during recession. The bigger challenge you have is creating a sense of urgency for innovation where things are going well and when sales are rising rapidly. So I would say the mindset of innovation, the culture of innovation and focus on innovation have to be constant whether your business is doing well or not; whether the economy is doing well or is in recession. In fact, I would say that the leaders will have to focus much more on innovation when the company is doing well. Maybe it is somewhat contrarian.

I believe our aspirations are our possibilities. The limit to the pace of innovation comes from our desire to distinguish ourselves from our competitors in the minds of our customers and to enhance our margins. Differentiation in the marketplace does not make sense unless you can get better margins than your competitors. As long as the leaders of a corporation—the CEO, the COO, the CFO, and other leaders—are focused on the need to differentiate in the marketplace, the innovation culture will be alive in the organization. The day the senior management forgets their focus on differentiation in the marketplace and on getting better margins, the spirit of innovation will disappear in the company. So, the pace of innovation is driven purely by the mindset of the senior management in the company, and by the focus on customers, and by the desire to get better margins. I would say it is really senior management that is the bottleneck or the source of strength for innovation.

What advice can you give other CEOs to advance innovation?

First of all, we have to create an environment of openness where any good idea coming from anybody, irrespective of the hierarchy, can be discussed, debated, and accepted. Second, we have to create an environment of meritocracy. All decisions will have to be taken based on data. There should not be any hysteresis of bias from prior transactions in the current transaction. That is, we have to start every transaction on a zero base so that youngsters are confident of winning the current transaction even though they lost the previous transaction. That is why we, at Infosys, celebrate the adage, "In God we trust, everybody else brings data to the table." Third, we have to encourage youth because youth is all about new ideas. Youth is about non-conventional ideas, youth is about energy, youth is about future, and youth is about enthusiasm. So, we have to create an environment where the young people are very confident, they are very energetic and they are very enthusiastic to add value to the corporation.

For example, we have a dedicated day called Innovation Day which we celebrate once a year. It could be one, two, or three days based on how many ideas are there. That day the only people who are allowed to stand up, speak, and make a presentation are people who are below 30 years of age. Everybody else has to simply listen and perhaps ask questions. So the good thing about the Innovation Day is it gives visibility to youngsters, it gives them confidence. It tells them that the organization respects youth and new ideas. We have to create incentives for people to innovate. That incentive could be money, recognition, or visibility. People do need incentives.

Innovation flourishes when innovators are in touch with customers. Often, we facilitate interaction between our customers and young researchers from our SETLabs (Software Engineering and Technology Laboratories). Unless our researchers realize what the outside world is and what is happening in the trenches, their innovations will have no value for the customer. This is how Infosys encourages every professional to think in terms of business value to the customer.

How can you improve business value to your customers?

In everything we do, we ask ourselves how we can improve speed, productivity, and quality; enhance excellence in execution, employee morale, customer satisfaction, and the bottom line for the company. This is how we add value to our customers. If we follow some of these things, we could improve the business value to our customers. But the most important requirement for innovation in a corporation is to create a culture of youth, openness, meritocracy, and receptivity to new ideas.

AFTERWORD
FUTURE INNOVATION CHALLENGES

Predictions are often another way to spell "guess." Nonetheless, several trends are likely to appear in a CEO's innovation agenda, as globalization, rapid technology cycles, and intensified competition increase pressures to improve innovative performance.

The Internet's ability to access knowledge resources, as well as connect with customers and suppliers, improves daily. The future promises to show more networking both in person and over the Web. Companies will seek to attract and engage human talent and specialized resources to improve innovation performance across a range of activities, such as R&D, business model development, marketing, and distribution.

A major question is the degree to which corporations will open corporate "walls" to engage external partners to advance innovation. Not only is this a cultural issue, but orchestrating multiple partners to cooperate over several years or more for major projects is not a simple matter. Companies will need to devote significant senior executive attention beyond negotiating initial terms and objectives to managing these partnerships.

Partnering, especially through open innovation, will introduce unexpected partners because research goals, rather than in-house capabilities, will identify the most promising research directions and capable resources. "What's going to change, in my view," says Cescau, "is that just like with globalization and the Internet, you're going to partner with people that in the past you would have had no idea you were going to partner with."

Sometimes a mindset change will be necessary. Fehrenbach notes that at Bosch:

> But the idea of cooperating with other companies that might also be your competitors later on is new. Other companies have no problem with such ventures. They set them up without delay, and later on they also share the work of manufacturing. But this is not the typical way Bosch does things, not the "Bosch DNA." Changing this will require a major paradigm shift.

Companies will explore new ways to improve R&D efficiency. As Buckley remarks about 3M:

> we have to find ways to become more efficient, to innovate faster and more efficiently ... the reality is that innovation is happening faster and faster everywhere in the world and, as a company who has made innovation its business, we have to learn to be faster.

Methods to improve R&D efficiency will inevitably involve changes in business management practices as executives learn and apply such techniques as more networking, open innovation, and simultaneous development of new business models and R&D. Designing novel business models in tandem with research priorities will be an increasingly popular and likely essential method linking research to market opportunities. For not only does synchronizing research and new business models help tighten research objectives, it offers the prospect to rewrite competitive rules.

For example, Kagermann, explaining why companies should not rely exclusively on product innovation, notes, "I think even as a very successful product innovator, you should ask yourself whether your future couldn't be a combination of a new product with a different business model, because that could really change the game."

New risk management techniques, including efforts to allocate resources more efficiently, will appear. Ironically, because of more rapid technology cycles, longer-term planning will be required to prepare for successive product or service generations in businesses that previously were accustomed to shorter planning schedules. Some industries, such as pharmaceuticals or automobiles, have always had long development gestations, while consumer product companies typically follow shorter R&D paths. However, when companies lengthen R&D development, greater coordination among participants, such as internal and external innovation resources, corporate strategy, marketing, and distribution will create new management challenges.

"We need to extend our planning horizon, which has all sorts of implications in terms of risk, in terms of number of bets, size of the bet, in terms of alignment," notes Cescau about Unilever's product development portfolio. "... It will require a very different stance for the management."

Management stress will only increase as executives try to develop innovation portfolio strategies that balance shorter-term incremental and longer-term breakthrough development paths in response to the relentless need for speed. As Fujio Cho remarks, "Without a slightest delay we have to invest human and financial resources to keep up with the speed of global markets. Yet, it seems that time is against us, forcing us to hurry even more."

To speed R&D and defray risks, collaboration for basic research among competitors will become more prevalent. Such collaborations will appear in industries that previously conducted fundamental research either independently or in association with academic institutions. Senior management will need to devote more attention to such relationships as antitrust and product development issues come to the fore.

The benefits of harnessing cultural diversity will become ever more apparent as companies that can leverage cultural diversity across R&D and marketing will likely experience higher growth than peers less facile in either internal or external transnational conversations. "That is why we are really focusing on diversity at Nokia," explains Kallasvuo. "We are following that, we are setting targets and planning quite a lot how we can increase our diversity."

Because innovations can be costly and their purpose is to improve corporate performance, there will be greater pressure to assess the potential of innovations to improve margins. This attention is beneficial, because "the day the senior management forgets their focus on differentiation in the marketplace and on getting better margins," predicts Murthy, "the spirit of innovation will disappear in the company .... I would say it is really senior management that is the bottleneck or the source of strength for innovation."

All companies will need a CEO who, in word and deed, is an innovation champion. The opportunities and risks are too great to assign innovation leadership responsibilities outside the CEO suite.

INDEX

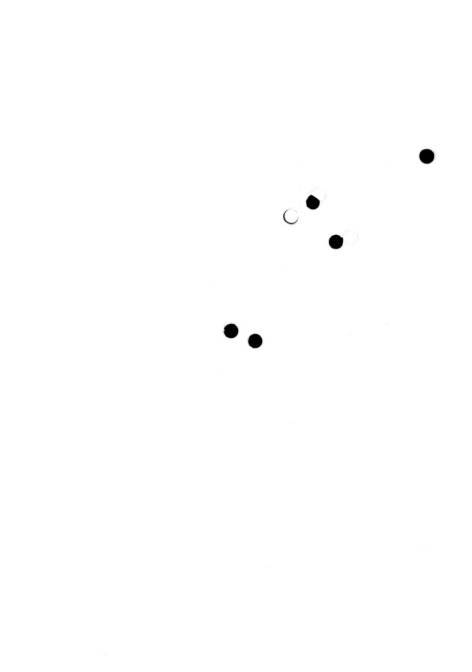